TIMED ENERGY

Understanding human behaviour past, present and future

Ian Senior

THE AUTHOR

Ian Senior was born in 1938. He was educated at the Dragon School, Oxford; Sedbergh School, Cumbria; Trinity College, Oxford, and University College London where he took an MSc (econ). An economic consultant for over 30 years, he has published numerous papers, articles and monographs on postal services, parallel trade in prescription medicines, the financial impact of theatre critics on the West End and, more recently, on corruption. His book *Corruption: the World's Big C* was published by the Institute of Economic Affairs and Profile Books in June 2006.

Ian Senior: *Time and Energy*

Published in September 2013 by emp3books Ltd
Norwood House, Elvetham Road, Fleet, GU51 4HL

©Ian Senior

The author asserts the moral right to be identified as the author of this work. All views are those of the author.

ISBN-13: 978-1-907140-79-2

SUMMARY

Ian Senior starts from two extremely simple concepts:
a) time and energy are two absolutes on which all economic activity is based; and
b) most humans are *economic* most of the time.

From these two premises he explains the activities of individuals, groups, societies and nations from the past through to the present and future.

The energy that has to be harnessed for most activity is no longer that of human muscles but comes from external energy, namely fossil fuels and to a lesser extent from atomic power, wind and water. The golden age of accessible and cheap fossil fuels is waning. This fact will influence every aspect of human activity from the number of years we work to the food and goods we produce.

Ian Senior shows how time and energy have influenced economic man in relation to war, religion, migration, democracy and human behaviour generally. He describes the effect on civilisation of waning fossil fuel energy. The reserves of oil and gas at current rates of consumption will last about 64 years. Coal reserves will last longer but will bring more pollution. Wind and water power cannot be expected to make up for reductions of oil and gas output. The safety of atomic power is still questionable in the light of Chernobyl and Fukushima. He argues that energy should be the currency of last resort and he proposes denominating currencies in terms of kilowatt hours as a way of giving money true value and of preventing delinquent governments from simply printing it.

This book gives a new understanding of the economics of time, energy and human behaviour presented in a clear and highly original way.

CONTENTS

Ian Senior: *Time and Energy*

PART 1
CONCEPTS

Ian Senior: *Time and Energy*

1   INTRODUCTION

This book is about ideas and is a search for understanding. Most of the ideas themselves are derived from observing the everyday world around us and can be tested by our experience and intuition. Of course these two are not infallible — intuition used to make people think the world flat, and our individual experience may be atypical — but they are useful starting points.

Ideas can be of immense power. They form the basis of philosophies and religions, for the way societies are organised and how people treat each other. So, when an idea becomes accepted by leaders and decision-makers the consequences are important, and when they are absorbed into societies' behaviour their impact becomes incalculable. For example, the impact of the world's major religions and of thinkers such as Adam Smith, Karl Marx and Mao Zedong are self-evident.

Ideas by their nature are the product of the mind and they precede action. If people were to act with no preconceived ideas of what they were about to do and why they proposed to do it, there would be no organised society. Man, because he can think at a very high level, is entirely distinct from other creatures. A few of these, for example ants and bees, have highly organised societies but the working of an ant-heap cannot be compared with the complex actions needed to build a washing machine including the provision of electricity to make it run, water to clean the clothes and drains to take away the waste water.

Man is distinguished from animals by three abilities:
- he thinks with great complexity;
- he communicates his thoughts to other men through speech and writing, and records his thoughts accurately for present and future use; and
- individually or in a group he translates thoughts into action.

In man thought comes before action but actions in turn influence the development of thought. For example, primitive man had the idea of cutting and made knives out of flint. Then he found that metal was a better cutting material. Thus the idea of cutting led to search for better ways of cutting that now include oxyacetylene torches, lasers and industrial explosives.

This book does not attempt to explain where man's ideas come from in the first place. That is the realm of many theories embodied in religion, metaphysics and science. Instead, it deals mainly with the ways these are translated into action.

Man is complex and many attempts have been made to categorise and explain the way he functions. I have used what I believe to be an original and useful classification. I consider man as having three dimensions: *economic, spiritual* and *sexual.* This book is mainly about economic man, but the other two dimensions are considered where they interact with economic man.

The words 'economic' and 'economical' are frequently used in everyday speech to mean using as little of a given input as possible to produce a required quantity of output. In the plural the term 'economics' means a branch of learning which concerns the way groups of people, sometimes called 'economies', are organised. Economists are social scientists who try to explain the causal relationships between the myriad activities of ordinary people. At a global or nationwide level *macro*-economics is the study of actions by governments on a range of measurable things such as production, consumption, investment, trading, inflation and the balance of payments. At the level of firms and individuals, *micro*-economics is the study of how markets operate and how people behave in relation to prices and other external circumstances such as actions by government.

This book is rooted in micro-economics but it is written for anyone to read. Indeed, it develops theories and arguments that will not be found in conventional economics textbooks — the influential but frequently inaccessible 'dismal science'. It recognises that not all activity is economic and so it also discusses the influence of *spiritual man* and *sexual man*. Both these aspects of man also influence the way individuals behave but in general they are less important in daily life than the need to put bread on the table, clothes on the body and a roof over the head which are the primary duties of economic man.

In this book I use the term 'economic' as a way of describing one particularly important dimension of man. I define 'economic' as meaning that part of man which is concerned with survival and satisfaction of economic needs. This simple concept means virtually the same thing as self-interest. The difference is that self-interest has overtones of selfishness which is thought to be a bad characteristic. 'Economic' on the other hand is a neutral word and therefore more useful for my purposes. Readers can mentally substitute 'self-interested' for 'economic' throughout the book if it helps them to test the theories I put forward.

The logic and arguments are intended to be pellucidly clear. Each chapter, each paragraph, almost each sentence is a link in the chain that can be tested by the reader's experience or intuition. The ideas appear strong enough to explain that dominating component of human behaviour, namely economic activity, and to have powerful implications for the future of mankind.

Throughout this book I use the terms man, men and mankind to mean both men and women. I am sorry if this upsets feminists and those who debate whether God is male or female, but it saves words and is quite clear.

The book starts from the assumption that most people are economic most of the time. Is this cynical? Does it put man on a par with animals who appear to be economic all the time except when they are sleeping, mating or protecting their young from predators? Does it conflict with the teachings of major religions and philosophies? Is it negated by the lives of people like Mother Theresa of Calcutta? Each reader must judge for himself but here is my starting point:

-      **Key concept No 1:** ***most people are economic most of the time.***

If you agree with this premise you will probably find that the book takes you logically to conclusions you did not expect. I do not suggest that all people are economic all the time, which clearly is untrue. However, spiritual people must regularly take economic actions. Eating is the most fundamental of economic actions and even saintly people have to eat though many are quite slim.

If you accept that most people are economic most of the time, this book provides a clear and original understanding of how and why most people behave most of the time. Examples are given based on observing economic man's actions past and present. The conclusions drawn can then be used to predict the future and to give guidance on decision-making at all levels of economic action from government through institutions to the actions of individuals at work, at leisure and at home.

Key concept No 2: *time and energy, taken together, fully explain the actions of economic man.*

In the next chapters I explain this more fully.

Ian Senior: *Time and Energy*

2   TIME, THE FIRST ABSOLUTE

Time and energy are two absolutes. Time as we know it is totally inflexible. If I set an accurate clock running I can measure the amount of time that passes. Two accurate clocks running in parallel record the same amount of time passing. Einstein's theory of relativity might imply some modification to the last statement but, for the purposes of normal human life, clocks accurately measure time.

Sometimes our perception of time varies. For example, when we are enjoying ourselves time seems to pass quickly and, conversely, when we are unhappy, waiting, in pain or bored, time seems to drag. In reality, the clocks carry on ticking at the same rate. Time for the purposes of this book is totally inflexible.

In the normal physical world time cannot be created, destroyed or transformed. This is not to deny the existence of a paranormal world. Descriptions of ghosts and other paranormal phenomena are too common for us to assume that they are all an elaborate confidence trick perpetrated over countless years by countless people in countless circumstances and for no obvious reason. Some research illustrates how even ordinary people may have access to different periods of time yet without disturbing the passing of time as we know it. Dunne (1927)[1] argues that when we dream we move into a new dimension of time which is at right-angles to time as we ordinarily know it. Normal time is experienced as though we are in a car driving along a road. We can remember and record things which we have passed and are behind us on the road, but we know nothing about the road around the corner in front of us. According to Dunne, when we dream it is as though we are in a helicopter hovering above the car. From the helicopter we can see the car travelling along the road, but we can see with equal clarity the road in front of the car as well as behind it. Thus our dreams are as likely to concern the future as the past.

Dunne's theory is powerful and has been neglected for too long. It was developed from his experience of powerful dreams and he carried out experiments to test the theory scientifically. Most dreams are quickly forgotten unless recorded immediately, and only the most powerful dreams are remembered for minutes, let alone days, after we have woken. Most of us can recall a few very powerful dreams we have had in our lives. Many people are aware of having had dreams, sometimes long and complex, almost every time they awake. However, unless dreams are recorded at once, all but a minute fraction of the evidence to test Dunne's theory is lost. In his experiment, groups of people wrote down their dreams immediately on waking. Dunne's findings were not conclusive but they lent some support to his theory. When I read Dunne's book and became more interested in dreams, I experienced some clear cases of dreaming about things, generally quite trivial events, that occurred a few days later.

There is nothing new in the concept of dreams as a means of prophesying the future. The Old Testament of the Bible provides examples such as that of Joseph, now widely known through the Lloyd-Webber and Rice musical *Joseph and His Amazing Technicolour Dreamcoat*.

---

[1]   Dunne, J. W. *An Experiment With Time*, Faber, London

Another field of experiment that concerns time is that of regression under hypnosis. Many examples of work in this field are given by Moss and Keeton (1979)[2] and Williston and Johnston (1988)[3]. These books set out to demonstrate that when certain people are under hypnosis, they can recall not only everything about their life to date including early childhood but also the act of being born and life in the womb. More than that, they can recall in detail lives they have lived before the present one. Frequent excerpts from verbatim transcripts are quoted in the books.

The concept of reincarnation, or the human spirit returning to live successive lives in different bodies and at different times, is an accepted part of Hinduism and Buddhism. It was part of the early Christians' beliefs but then was dropped from official teaching. Despite this, belief in reincarnation is strongly held by some practising Christians.

The nature of hypnosis is little understood. Its popularity as stage entertainment is sometimes jeopardised when people who have been hypnotised experience unwanted side-effects afterwards. The work of a stage hypnotist reveals the extraordinary way that individuals can be changed instantaneously from their normal selves into completely different characters and back again by the hypnotist's simple commands. In the stage shows of Paul McKenna, for many years a personable and popular stage hypnotist, people under hypnosis

---

2   Moss.P, and J. Keeton, *Encounters with the Past. Astonishing Accounts of Hypnotic Regression,* Sidgwick and Jackson; Penguin Books, 1981

3   Williston, G. and J Johnstone *Discovering your past lives. Spiritual growth through a knowledge of past lifetimes.* The Aquarian Press, London, 1988. First published as *Soul search,* 1983.

mingled freely with the audience during the interval, talking lucidly like good actors playing the role assigned to them by the hypnotist. I have spoken to some of his subjects after a performance and they had a clear recollection of what they were doing under hypnosis. This is supposed to be a safeguard that prevents the hypnotist from forcing them to act against their will, but even this freedom of choice is uncertain.

Evidently hypnosis acts upon the brain and makes it send commands to the body to carry out abnormal actions. Given that the brain is the site of memory it seems plausible that hypnosis is able to unlock memories that in the normal state are inaccessible.

The implications of hypnosis, like Dunne's theory, are so profound that it seems surprising how little research takes place compared, for example, with other forms of behaviour including the experience of pain. Stage subjects under hypnosis can cry out in pain if they are told that something they are holding is hot, and the obverse is possible. A few dentists use hypnosis on their patients as an alternative to injections. It would be practical if patients could themselves switch off pain at will and this appears to be possible among people who have practised meditation for many years. Self-hypnotic experiments have been successfully carried out in the west in which ordinary people with little instruction have learned to walk over burning coals without pain or after-effects.

Self-hypnosis might be a way of improving access to our memories. The learning process is a method of putting facts and concepts into our memories in such a way that they can be recalled at will. However, only a tiny fraction of what we put into our memories can later be recalled. I may remember what I ate yesterday but I cannot remember what I ate a week ago unless it was outstandingly good or bad or linked to something else I can easily remember such as a significant conversation or event. Many people recall accurately what they were doing when they heard that President Kennedy had been shot.

The question of the brain's power to store information revolves around whether information in the memory fades like an old photograph until it no longer exists or whether it is always there, indelibly stored as in a filing cabinet that has been trundled into the archives where the contents cannot be accessed without the help of an archivist.

A further issue is whether the files in the brain which come out of the archives under hypnosis are true recollections of personal experience; or recollections of what the person has read or heard; or whether they include recollections inherited genetically at birth along with other characteristics passed on through the parents' genes. When people under hypnosis recall childhood it is often possible to verify their recollections quite easily. It is less easy to verify their accounts of previous lives but it can be done, sometimes with remarkable confirmation by scholars of the accuracy of descriptions concerning events that took place centuries earlier.

The books I have mentioned present compelling evidence to support the credibility of previous lives recalled under hypnosis. I have also been present when a hypnotherapist asked a subject under hypnosis to describe what was happening to her in a past life. Most people under hypnotic regression can recall several lives, sometimes with historical detail that could not have been gained from the subject's own reading. Sometimes the subjects remember nothing of what they had said under hypnosis and on regaining consciousness may dispute the factual accuracy of events they recounted under hypnosis. Others are aware of what they are saying when, under hypnosis, they describe a previous life. There are varying depths of hypnotic trance and possibly it is in the deeper levels that subjects are no longer aware of what they are saying in answer to the hypnotist's questions.

These books and others like them are based on transcripts of recordings made during sessions of hypnotic regression. The evidence which has been compiled in this way is compelling. The reader cannot avoid making one of three judgements. The first possibility is that the books are an elaborate confidence trick. This is implausible because observers have been present at the sessions and there are several books that describe specific examples of hypnotic regression with considerable similarity.

The second possible explanation is that the accounts of previous lives by subjects under hypnosis are drawn from information they have read earlier and now forgotten. However, many of the cases given in the books make this implausible. The verbal transcripts of the subjects have the ring of personal observation rather than of tracts of reading material recalled for the occasion.

The third possible explanation is that the accounts are drawn from some form of collective subconscious acquired by heredity. This implies that anyone under hypnosis with common ancestry could draw on the same collection of experiences. It is an explanation that raises as many difficulties as it resolves. An explanation that depends on one hypothesis is normally more telling than one that depends on several. In fact the simplest and most compelling explanation is that the recollections of subjects under hypnosis are genuine accounts of events that happened to them in previous lives. Just as normally I cannot recall something mundane such as what I had for breakfast a week ago, so it seems equally plausible that I can have forgotten a mundane life completed many years ago before my present one.

A striking feature of the transcripts is that commonly the subject describes events in the present tense as though they are happening there and then. This reinforces the concept of time-warp. Much less common in the transcripts are descriptions of *future* lives. One such is found in *Discovering Your Past Lives.*[4]. In this, the subject named Robert describes himself in a future life:

> "I see him in the San Francisco of your future after the rebuilding of the city...A devastating earth movement has destroyed much of the area and Robert lost everything but his great gift of music..." Robert later defined the date of this future life as 2085.

According to the accounts of these books, the number of years as we know them that elapse between reincarnations is variable, commonly with centuries in between. The concept of reincarnation by the soul leaving one body and *immediately* entering another is not supported by the work of these authors. However, plenty of cases relate to earlier lives only a century or so ago, so it would seem reasonable to

---

[4]   Willistone, G. and J Johnstone, *op cit*, p216

expect to find subjects living today who will experience further lives a century from now. The prospects for learning about the future are tantalisingly available and it would miss an extraordinary opportunity if practitioners of hypnotic regression did not place equal or more emphasis on the future rather than the past.

Another author who questions the nature of time as we know it is Manning (1978)[5], a contemporary medium. In *The Strangers* he gives a detailed account of a ghost, a former owner of the house in which the author and his family were living. Manning saw the ghost on several occasions and held long written conversations with him in which Manning asked questions and the ghost replied in writing through Manning's hand. The book includes a photograph of a wall on which the signatures of the ghost's many contemporaries appeared at different times and who Manning was able to authenticate through the parish records. In some conversations with the ghost, it became clear that the ghost was living in his own present time, describing his painful legs, for example, and unaware of Manning's existence.

I have instanced these books to show that we do not necessarily understand the nature of time. All of them suggest that time is not necessarily sequential but possibly multidimensional or omnipresent. However, I also wish to stress that such studies of the paranormal in no way affect my premise that time as we know it is an absolute constraint on human activity. Time-warps may occur in dreams or under hypnosis but the subjects in question are not carrying out economic activity at the moments concerned. Therefore they cannot be described as economic men at the time. If they remember their

---

[5] Manning. M, *The Strangers*. W H Allen, London

dreams they might change their actions the following day, for example, deciding to cancel a passage on the Titanic. However, few people give credence to the content of dreams or write them down immediately on wakening. They may be mocked if they take specific actions in response to their dreams, so any economic impact arising from a time-warp approach to dreams and to hypnotic regression can be thought of as small and extremely difficult to measure in any scientific way.

In essence, if all the phenomena I have mentioned were fully understood and accepted as fact, I believe that clocks would still run conventionally while economic man was producing and consuming. Similarly, the scope, shape and nature of Einstein's concept of time will have no impact on our daily economic activity. Economic man remains firmly anchored in time as we know it. He experiences the passing of time and measures it by clocks. Clocks, for the purposes of this book, are a necessary, sufficient and accurate representation of the reality of time — a dimension which economic man cannot influence any more than an ant can influence the length of a ruler on which it is walking.

3   ENERGY, THE SECOND ABSOLUTE

Energy is the second of the two absolutes. Energy, like time, lies entirely outside man. This may not be immediately obvious and needs explanation.

Humans possess no energy of their own but instead capture it from other sources. Food is the energy that maintains our bodies, some of which comes directly from plant life. Other food derives from animals, fish and birds which in turn obtain their food from eating other creatures or vegetable matter. Ultimately all food therefore comes from vegetable matter. It is obvious that without food, the primary source of energy, human and animal life would cease.

Unlike time, however, energy is something that can be transformed in many ways. The human body transforms food to enable the body to grow, renew itself and to provide energy which the body needs to function at all. Natural energy can also be transformed using mechanisms devised by man. For example, water can turn a wheel which generates electricity. This can be transformed through an electric motor into mechanical power to turn another wheel which itself moves water. In the latter case mechanical energy *from* water has been transformed twice to produce mechanical energy *upon* water.

Although energy can be transformed and can be dissipated as heat, it cannot be destroyed. This truth is known to scientists but perhaps requires explanation. Energy from oil, for example, is not created: it is released as heat when oil burns. Heat can be transformed into mechanical energy and when this happens some part of it is

19

dissipated and cannot be used or recovered. Mechanical friction, as in the case of a wheel turning on an axle, becomes heat which is lost to the atmosphere. Similarly when an electrical current passes through a wire it meets resistance and part of the energy is transformed into heat which is lost to the atmosphere. All heat ultimately is lost to the atmosphere and for human purposes ceases to be useful.

The nearest that man comes to *creating* energy is through causing chemical or nuclear reactions. In this context man finds a way to release energy that is latent in the materials concerned. Fire is the simplest example. However, man does not create fire; he creates the conditions in which the latent energy in a material such as coal or oil can be released as heat through combustion.

The proportion of energy lost when it is harnessed or transformed can be considerable. When coal is burned in a power station roughly two thirds of the energy is lost as irrecoverable heat and only one third is harnessed via turbines as electricity. Scientists and engineers have constantly sought to increase the proportion of energy harnessed and to reduce the wasted heat but energy will always ultimately be lost into the atmosphere as heat. The best that the scientists and engineers can do is to reduce the proportion of wastage. They still have far to go. For example, an efficiently insulated building could use the sun to maintain a living temperature. Instead, houses in cold climates leak heat and consume constant supplies of new energy as heat to keep their occupants comfortable. In summer some have air-conditioning that requires energy to run. Thus, in both hot weather and cold, energy is spent keeping humans within a comfortable range of temperatures.

Some energy is intentionally wasted as heat. Power stations have vast towers in which hot water is cooled by the atmosphere. The radiators of cars have an identical function. A perfect car would transform all the petrol's energy into movement and none into heat. In this context a radiator and a cooling system would be unnecessary and exhaust fumes would be emitted at the same temperature as the air originally sucked into the system. Major improvements in battery technology have meant that partly or fully electric cars are beginning to become commercially viable. Even so, electricity has to be generated in the first place and the current debate rages about whether natural sources such as wind, waves or biomass fuels can produce enough electricity to replace fossil fuels as they run down.

The industrial revolution began with the discovery that steam energy could be transformed into mechanical energy. This mechanical energy in turn could be used to do things that humans, using their own muscles, could not. The discovery of steam energy produced a chain reaction of activity in which human energy became less important and external energy became more so.

The world's resources of coal were abundant and initially were more than enough to satisfy the needs of industry. The abiding legacy of steam is the world's network of railways even though over the past decades steam locomotives have been replaced by those powered by electricity or diesel.

It is extraordinary to recall, however, that the railways themselves, like the canals which preceded them, were constructed entirely by manual effort — navvies with picks, shovels and wheelbarrows. Horses and carts could move soil but men, with hard toil, levelled the ground, dug the tunnels, built the embankments and bridges and laid the sleepers and rails. Think of this when you next dig your garden for an hour and then again when you travel by train!

Leaving aside railway locomotives, steam ships, traction engines and steam rollers, steam provided energy in mainly static situations such as factories and mills. Steam locomotion was impossible over rough country.

The discovery of mineral oil and the invention of the internal combustion engine provided a quantum leap forward in the application of nature's energy to man's needs. The immediate improvement lay in the very compact size of an internal combustion engine and its fuel compared with the size and weight of a steam engine with comparable output of power. The internal combustion engine enabled the invention of lorries, mechanical excavators, bulldozers, cranes and all the machines that have been used to construct vast networks of roads, airports, cities, skyscrapers and buildings of every sort.

The discovery of electricity in the nineteenth century was first applied to lighting. Later in the century came the invention of the electric motor enabling electricity to be used as a source of mechanical energy. The characteristic of electricity as mechanical energy initially was similar to steam in being difficult to transmit to where it was needed. Additionally, like steam power, it was difficult to store it until needed.

The modern ability to transmit electricity over long distances together with the development of electric motors of all sizes made the application of electric power universal as a substitute for human effort. Washing machines, dishwashers and vacuum cleaners replaced the manual housework previously done by housewives or servants. Batteries for storage of electricity remain heavy though important improvements are being made, not least under the pressure of declining reserves of oil and the attractions of silent, non-polluting vehicles.

From earliest days, man has sought ways of harnessing nature's energy to replace manual effort. Wind and water energy had been harnessed by man for hundreds of years in the form of windmills and watermills, but the amount of instant, predictable and controllable energy they could produce, particularly in the case of windmills, was far less than the energy that could be derived from fossil fuels when converted directly into heat or indirectly into electricity and hence into mechanical energy. Water-driven turbines are still important power generators in Switzerland, for example, and dams are still built elsewhere to produce electricity but the easiest sources of water energy have been exploited.

Fossil fuel
In addition to coal, the main fossil fuels are oil and natural gas. Other forms of fossil fuel are lignite (a form of soft coal), tar and oil-shale. These fuels have lower energy content and require more processing to extract energy in the form of heat. Gas includes natural gas and "town gas" which is derived from coal.

A modern technique known as 'fracking' is still in early stages but offers the possibility to extract natural gas from geological formations that are not wells and are on land. The risk of pollution from the pressurised liquid that is used to force the gas out and the possibility of earth tremors caused by the process are still being debated with scientists and engineers on one side and green associations on the other.

The common characteristic of all fossil fuel is that its origin is vegetation — mainly trees — that grew millions of years ago, died, fell and in many cases were covered up by movements of the earth's crust. Over millions of years and under heavy pressure this vegetation became transformed into fossil fuel.

Most forms of vegetation burn when dry: wood, stalks, leaves, peat and even fruit and vegetables. Human and animal tissue also burns when dry, as people know who have burned the Sunday joint. Because their water content has been eliminated fossil fuels have a much higher energy content for a given weight or mass than other combustible materials. For example, one kilo of coal produces far more heat than one kilo of wood.

It is important to note that electricity is *not* a primary source of energy because it is produced from fossil fuels, hydro or wind power. It would become a primary source only if ways were found to capture and store lightning.

When man discovered that coal provided much more energy than wood it became the obvious choice for creating warmth, cooking and for simple industrial purposes. Initially coal was used solely to produce heat for warmth and then, much later, for melting ores to produce metals such as gold, silver and bronze. However, the discovery of steam power created an enormous new demand for coal and in little time coalmining became a major industrial activity. Depending on how the earth's crust had moved over millions of years, coal seams were found at the surface or underground. Humans like to economise personal energy, so the first mines were those where coal was easiest to extract.

In the early days of mining in the nineteenth century, steam power was impracticable for work underground and the internal combustion engine and electric motor had not been invented. Even when both had been invented, they were not immediately suited to mining because both steam and internal combustion engines must vent to atmosphere, which is difficult in the context of mines. So in the early days the quest for natural energy, coal mining required much human energy, mainly men with picks and shovels like those who built roads, canals and railways. Ponies were used in some pits for moving coal and so were women. Children were used to open and shut doors in the mines.

The application of efficient electric motors came later. They required no venting to atmosphere but were not ideal to use because they generated sparks that were dangerous in the context of coal mines where flammable gas was a permanent hazard. A later development was pneumatic power in which compressors driven by electric motors converted electric energy into compressed air that powered pneumatic drills.

Despite these advances the work in mines for a hundred years was appalling by modern standards. Even so, people worked freely in them, drawn by higher wages than for other forms of manual work. Sweated labour they may have been but forced labour they were not.

25

The quest for energy was so strong that people worked down the mines willingly and do so, though in much reduced numbers, to the present day. Indeed, the violent miners' strike that racked the UK in 1984-85 was more an attempt by the miners to prevent the closure of mines than about the conditions of working in them.

The nineteenth century saw the start of the systematic mining of coal while the twentieth century saw the advent of the internal combustion engine, the car, lorry and later the plane, all of which dramatically increased demand for oil-based derivatives. The process of oil extraction became increasingly easy because internal combustion engines and electricity were now available for drilling, extracting and transporting the product to sites where it was processed for industrial and consumers' consumption. Whereas coal, when converted into steam power at the surface, did not make mining much easier apart from working the lifts to take miners down the pit, the availability of oil as a motive force for electricity produced powerful drilling rigs and pumps that extracted more oil faster from yet deeper wells. Thus the acceleration in extracting fossil fuels took place because of man's ability to transform fossil fuels — oil, gas and coal — into electricity and hence into mechanical energy.

Cheap energy

The era of cheap energy based mainly on fossil fuels began with the industrial revolution in the early nineteenth century and is past its peak today. Hydro energy is cheaper than fossil fuel because once a dam has been built there are virtually no production costs and the mechanical power of the turbines can be converted directly into electricity. Hydroelectricity entails the damming of rivers to store the power of the water that turns the turbines. The availability of suitable sites is limited and the side-effects on people and the ecology have to be considered. The most obvious sites for hydro power in Europe, for example in Switzerland, have already been developed.

In the nineteenth century there was no shortage of coal. The problem was to bring it to the surface and distribute it. Energy from wind and water could not be transported. Instead the emergence of coal as a source of mechanical energy rather than just heat, meant that for the first time energy could be brought to the user instead of the user going to the energy. Coal was relatively easy to distribute using horses, carts, barges and, later, railways and ships. The transport network, notably roads and rail, was driven forward by the need to bring coal to factories and to consumers.

In the nineteenth century, once coal had reached the place of transformation into secondary energy, namely steam, the onward distribution of mechanical energy was cumbersome. Steam engines in factories used complex systems of pulleys, gears and belts. There was no way of transferring mechanical energy to houses, so, at a time when factories were capable of producing goods from cotton, wool and steel, household chores were still done manually. Coal was carried to fireplaces in each room, clothes and dishes were washed by hand and floors were swept with brooms.

In the countryside the need for physical labour continued with little change. Steam driven vehicles were unsuitable for most activities in the fields. An exception was steam-driven machines with a belt that could be coupled, for example, to stationary threshers. In the UK up to the 1950s horses drew carts, ploughs and machines for sowing and reaping, but early machinery could not lift potatoes from the ground, bundle hay or trim hedges. Thus the industrial revolution of the nineteenth century was driven forward by steam energy. However, agriculture was transformed by the arrival of the internal combustion engine. In the early part of the twentieth century agricultural work was so hard that labourers were happy to volunteer for the First World War in order to get away from the fields.[6]

The internal combustion engine has removed much manual effort on the land, while the electric motor has removed much manual labour from the house. Our forebears would have envied our ability to press one switch to boil a kettle instead of having to make a fire; they would have relished the efficiency of a vacuum cleaner compared with the broom; and they would have been incredulous that today many people use electric razors and electric toothbrushes since both these activities require little personal energy.

Because economic man became more efficient at finding and extracting fossil fuel and at generating electricity from it, energy became cheaper. As a result he consumed more of it. Indeed a measure of his wealth became closely associated with the amount of energy he consumed. A wealthy man now has a large centrally heated house and possesses many domestic machines that consume energy — washing machines, dryers, dishwashers, cookers, ovens, microwave ovens, blenders, televisions and audio equipment; and of course one or more cars. Two cars per family are common, one for the husband's commute, the other for the school run and shopping.

---

[6]   See, for example Blythe.R, *Akenfield, Portrait of an English Village*, Penguin Books Ltd,1973

The increasing consumption of energy accelerated the search for oil and gas. These two fossil fuels have major advantages over coal: their energy content is as high as coal and they are far easier to extract and transport. Oil and gas usually gush from the well under their own pressure. Oil can readily be transported by pipe, lorry or ship. Gas, when liquefied can be transported similarly. Coal, however, does not flow along a pipe or transfer easily between containers. Still less does it force itself obligingly to the earth's surface.

Thus oil and gas became the preferred sources of primary energy. As they replaced coal for generating electricity and as a source of heat in the home, energy to industrial and domestic consumers became cheaper, stimulating demand further. A self-reinforcing cycle of increasing energy demand and supply set in. Then in the 1950s scientists began to do disturbing calculations. The world's reserves of fossil fuel, notably oil and gas, could be estimated though not accurately since new reserves continued to be found. The rate of consumption then and now was known and could be forecast with reasonable accuracy, and so the date of exhaustion under stated assumptions could be predicted within defined confidence limits.

Part 3 of this book describes the way in which the world's resources of fossil fuel, in particular oil and gas, are being used up and discusses the prospects for expanding nuclear power. Renewable forms of energy such as wind and tidal water are obviously attractive for green reasons at a time when carbon emissions — the natural consequence of burning fossil fuel — are widely believed to be a primary cause of climate change. But the fundamental truth, which must not be obscured by the accuracy or inaccuracy of energy supply and demand forecasts, is this:

> *Man's personal supply of energy consists solely of his muscles. Otherwise he has no energy of his own.*

The future well-being of man, indeed his survival, depends entirely upon his capturing and harnessing energy which is not of his making and which derives from elements that he happens to find on Planet Earth. Reserves of fossil fuel are a finite resource and are becoming increasingly expensive as total supplies diminish and the cost of extracting them, often from the sea-bed, increases. Alternative sources such as wind, hydro, waves and biofuels from industrial alcohol and sugar cane, are limited by conditions such as the availability of sites on which to farm the vegetation. Solar energy is limitless but capturing it efficiently is still at an early stage.

Currently the world has seen the end of nearly two centuries of cheap fossil-fuel energy. The prices of oil and gas are climbing and will continue to do so. Risks associated with nuclear energy have been highlighted by the Chernobyl and Fukushima disasters. Even assuming that nuclear generation can become far safer, the disposal and storage of spent nuclear fuel remains a problem that scientists and engineers are far from solving. In a nutshell, cheap fossil-fuel energy has gone for good and potential replacements are fraught with technical problems still to be resolved.

4 THE RELATIONSHIP BETWEEN TIME AND ENERGY

People are continually aware of the constraints imposed by time and energy and try to economise both. For the most part instinct guides them. When we walk between two points we normally choose the shortest, flattest way in order to save both time and energy. If we can complete a task more quickly, we save time. If we do it more efficiently, say by reducing friction in a machine, we save energy. Often we trade energy off against time. Cars use more petrol over a given distance when they go faster, in which case saving time means consuming more energy.

An interesting phenomenon is that energy also naturally conserves itself. An electric current automatically chooses the path of least resistance through a circuit, and all systems of distributing electrical energy and of digital technology depend on this fact. Similarly, water flows more readily through a large hole than a small one.

Many important units of measurement relate time and energy: for example kilowatts per hour or barrels of oil per day. Using such units, men can measure the relative efficiency of different activities needed to achieve a defined end. Historically, most technological advance has been made with the intention of saving *human* time and energy. Machines are invented for this purpose. Domestic machines and industrial equipment all save human time or human energy in the form of labour, or both. Similarly, the prime function of transport is to save *human* time and energy. People use cars, trains and planes rather than walk or cycle. Walking and cycling can be for fitness, leisure and pleasure but, in terms of the distances covered and the time taken, recreational walking and cycling are a pinprick compared with normal travel.

Despite the finite nature of oil, natural gas and coal, only a tiny part of research effort seeks to increase the efficiency with which we consume natural energy. Much more is spent on seeking new oil and gas fields than on using existing energy better. Man has always been concerned with finding new ways to conserve his own energy rather than that of nature. Until recently all but a tiny minority of consumers preferred consumption to conservation. For reasons which are discussed in part 3 of this book, we must now find ways drastically to conserve non-human energy on this planet.

5   LAND, WATER, MINERALS AND OTHER FINITE RESOURCES

Land provides food, fresh water and raw materials for transformation into goods. Although the world's land mass is finite it does not yet represent a binding constraint on man's development. Large tracts of the world are still sparsely inhabited. Given time and energy, these parts could become habitable. Deserts could flower if economic man wanted to irrigate them and had the water to do so.

Land, like energy, is a resource which can be transformed in many ways. The mineral deposits it contains can be transformed into steel, other metals, cement and innumerable chemicals. Other parts of it can be rearranged to be useful. Stones can be built into walls and slates into roofs. When in short supply, land can be used intensively by building skyscrapers as in New York, Hong Kong and Singapore. When it is not in short supply it can be left as open space for cultivation, grazing, forestry or recreation.

Land differs from energy as a resource. Unlike fossil energy it can be used in many ways over time. It can be built on and it can be harvested many times year after year, but it remains a fragile resource. Intense cultivation reduces the yield, sometimes to almost nothing.

Before man's invention of chemical and nuclear weapons the permanency of land as the source of life was unquestioned. Today, there is no such certainty. The only certainty is that should man succeed in destroying himself by intention or accident, land will ultimately renew itself though it may take centuries or millennia to do so.

Land will always be essential to economic man. To fulfil his aspirations economic man constantly tries to gain control of land and of energy. He cannot control time but he can and does control the treatment of land and the energy he spends doing so. He can rent a field from its owner and decide what crops to plant and which machinery to buy. Similarly he can rent a house for a month and he can heat it using ten KW per hour of electricity throughout the period. Alternatively, for the same total cost he can rent the house longer and heat it with less electricity. In the same house he can install a machine that makes 100 units in one hour using 10 kilowatts of electricity or he may prefer a larger machine making 200 units per hour using 15 kilowatts. Many trade-offs are possible in the way man uses time, energy and land.

Time, energy and land are a hierarchy of constrains upon economic man. For man as an individual, time is an absolute constraint, whereas the availability of energy and land is constrained by social, economic and political factors. For the human race, time is not a constraint. However, the rising world population means that the availability and allocation of land will increasingly become a significant constraint. Energy is already a constraint and will increasingly become so as fossil fuels run short.

The sea is a counterpart to land and is becoming a resource that men dispute. Coastal waters are useful for fishing. Deep-sea waters are generally regarded as international but are increasingly becoming a source of dispute when they are believed to cover oil, gas or valuable minerals.

Two reasons explain why to date the sea has generated far less conflict between men compared with conflicts relating to land. The first is that the sea is a relatively minor source of food or energy. There have been disputes about the ownership of fishing rights, but only on rare occasions have these disputes caused bloodshed. There have also been disputes over the ownership of key sea approaches to land, such as the gulfs of Suez and Aqaba in the Red Sea which are of key commercial importance to Egypt and Israel respectively. However, these disputes are exceptional, and providing that non-coastal waters are available to all international shipping, there is little demand for ownership of the sea in terms of water. Land is a necessity. The sea is an asset but not a necessity for man's survival. Land-locked countries such as Switzerland manage to prosper without it.

Like all other resources, land is one which can be used economically or wasted thoughtlessly. The transformation of fertile land into waste-land in Africa and elsewhere has sometimes been caused by overgrazing and drought. In parts of South America, West Africa and Malaysia rain forests that have taken thousands of years to grow are destroyed in weeks or months. Until people in these countries learn to conserve the value of the land and its vegetation as their heritage they will be trapped in the vicious circle of urgently requiring more food from more over-worked land. They will repeat the mistakes which already have reduced the quantity and quality of land available to feed them. It takes a hundred years for a tropical tree to reach maturity and ten minutes to fell. The floods that put one third of Bangladesh under water in 1988 are attributed to erosion caused by deforestation.

We in the west are little wiser. Although most western democracies have come to recognise the value of the environment and are beginning to protect the land, we are squandering oil and gas in the same way that third world countries are squandering rainforests. Africans and others are more to be excused because they need the prime necessity of life, food, which in the west is abundant. Further, rainforests could regenerate themselves in a few centuries. Oil and gas cannot be regenerated.

In the earliest days of man's evolution, land was abundant but largely hostile. Primitive man had only his bare hands and rudimentary tools with which to tame the land. Some land possessed natural food in the form of fruit, vegetables and nuts. Other land was good hunting territory. Land that provided food or game was therefore the only resource to enable the continued existence of early man, and this remains true today in some third-world countries. Individual men therefore laid claim to the best areas of land and enclosed them when possible. Since land was the ultimate form of real wealth, man fought his neighbours for it. Territorial instinct was founded in the will to survive and remains as deep-seated as ever. Warfare became the standard way of acquiring or retaining land rights. From pre-history to the industrial revolution of the nineteenth century there was one simple truth:

—   *land provided food and food provided human energy.*

The industrial revolution changed the formula fundamentally. Land as a source of food remained important, but land was even more valuable if it contained coal and minerals that could be transformed using coal's energy. Because of steam power the manual work of labourers and craftsmen was taken over by machines that could spin, weave and produce finished goods previously made by hand.

The value of land therefore changed according to the value of its energy content. A given hectare of land with coal became far more valuable than an equivalent area of prime agricultural land. In the 20th and 21st centuries the discovery of oil and natural gas had the same effect. Some deserts, previously valueless, became massive sources of oil and gas. Their owners became billionaires overnight for having done precisely nothing.

The invention of the internal combustion engine produced a second industrial revolution and a new migration of people into cities and away from the land. Tractors replaced horses for ploughing and combined harvesters replaced horse-drawn reapers. From the industrial revolution onwards the new truth became:

—   some *land provided natural energy which in turn provided food and goods.*

By contrast with land, the sea has until recently not been thought of as a source of energy. Initially it was a source of food but only a minor one. The harnessing of fossil energy into power for fishing boats is exactly parallel to fossil fuel's use for farming. Without such power fishing would have remained the haphazard occupation it was when fishing-boats were propelled by sails.

The concept of territorial fishing rights is recent. It results from man's invention of ways of fishing the seas dry. When it became clear that modern fishing technology was capable of reducing fish stocks to the point of extinction, fishing rights became of great importance particularly to nations where fish is part of the staple diet. International laws were passed defining coastal rights. The EU has a common fisheries policy that is becoming as contentious as the common agricultural policy. The European Commission sets quotas for the amount and type of fish that each nation can catch from defined areas of the sea.

As a source of energy, the sea's potential is still largely untried. The harnessing of tidal power and wave power is just beginning. At present it is unlikely that there will be international conflict over the sea as a source of energy. Systems to capture tidal or wave energy will be coastal where territorial rights are clearly defined. Also it is improbable that if one nation captures sea energy in one place, this will reduce the sea's energy available for other nations.

However, the sea covers major deposits of oil, gas and minerals. For this reason areas of sea which hitherto were of no economic interest to nation states are become increasingly valuable. The bed of the south Atlantic around the Falkland Islands, for example, is believed to contain important oil and mineral deposits. If so, it will be like the deserts in the Arabian Gulf. It will have high value for a short period in history. When the oil or minerals have been extracted the sea bed will revert to desert once again.

Man's territorial instinct is primeval and stems from his need for food and his greed for energy. Food is necessary for survival; energy is necessary for comfort. Modern man has come to expect both. He will fight to gain or retain both land and sea which yield food and energy. Land will remain the prime source of food and the easiest source of fossil energy. The sea could provide more food than at present, provided that conservation and breeding of fish stocks take place, but it is harder to farm. The seabed is vast but harder to exploit. Man will be compelled to explore the seabed for energy and minerals at ever greater depths. As minerals on dry land become exhausted economic man, in his relentless quest for more energy and more wealth deriving from it, will turn his attentions even more to the sea and the seabed.

Ian Senior: *Time and Energy*

6   ECONOMIC MAN AND SPIRITUAL MAN

Man is a complex creature. Darwin's theory that man is descended from the apes by the survival of the fittest shocked those in his generation who believed that man was created directly by God. Cynics and humorists have described man as: an animal who eats when he isn't hungry, drinks when he isn't thirsty and who makes love in all seasons.

I suggest that man can usefully be analysed using three dimensions: economic, spiritual and sexual.   The intellectual concept of dimensions is that each must be completely distinct from the other. The mathematical concept is that dimensions are always at right angles to each other however many there are.

Taking three dimensions is convenient because we are accustomed to thinking in terms of three dimensions: length, breadth and height. These three dimensions, like the three dimensions by which I analyse man, meet at an origin and each is at 90 degrees to the other as in the diagram below. The origin can be thought of as the corner of a box. A speck of dust suspended in the air somewhere in the box can have its position defined by measuring its distance from the origin on each of the three dimensions. Similarly, an individual's personality can be defined by the three dimensions, economic, spiritual and sexual.

Let us scale each of the dimensions from 0 to 10. Here are examples of three individuals.   A pope may score 10 on the spiritual dimension, 2 on the economic dimension and one on the sexual though historically that as not always the case. A Casanova may score 10 on the sexual dimension, 7 on the economic dimension and one on the spiritual. A business tycoon may score 10 on the economic dimension and 5 on each of the other two. Any person can be positioned in the space defined by these three axes. His position in space is likely to vary as his age and other circumstances change.

The concept of analysing people's attributes according to these three dimensions may seem strange but in practice is plausible, convenient and useful. Everyone can be thought of as a combination of the three different dimensions.

The three dimensions of man are at right angles to each other

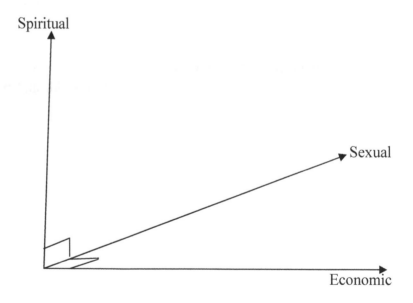

Now let us describe the three dimensions.

Economic man

Economic man is a consumer of resources. His actions concern the satisfaction of his body and are directed by the five senses. First and foremost his body requires food, clothing and shelter. In order to obtain these, economic man seeks territorial rights, possessions and the power to command services provided by others. In the earliest days when economic man won possession of land, he did so in order to obtain food. He also acquired shelter because the land was his to build on. If the land was larger than he needed for his own food, he allowed others to work the land and in return they gave him part of the produce. Thus, economic man seeks the power to command goods and services from others.

Spiritual man

Spiritual man comprises mind and emotions. He thinks, he loves, he hates. He is aware of beauty and of ugliness, of kindness and unkindness, of good and evil. He is not directly interested in whether these attributes provide satisfaction to his body or power over others. Of course professionally creative people such as artists, writers and musicians are happiest when their spiritual creativity is rewarded in economic terms but cases can be found in history of spiritual people living in garrets in order to fulfil their creativity or their vocation.

Sexual man

Sexual man is the simplest of the three dimensions. In its basic form sexuality is lust which requires satisfaction. At a higher level, sexuality takes the form of love as experienced by most people at some time and in different ways during their lives. Being in love and loving are two different aspects of the same emotion. Being in love is transitory. Loving is more durable but like all emotions it is an unstable condition.

Sexuality in man and animals is explained easily by Darwinism. If there was no procreation, races and species of men and animals would die out. In general, the male of the species pursues the female and fights off competitors. Pub fights over women have their parallels in lions and stags fighting to retain mating rights over a group of females.

Siting individuals along the three dimensions

Everyone can be sited on the three dimensions. Priests, monks and nuns must be assumed to be far from the origin along the spiritual dimension. They may not be at zero on the sexual dimension. They may take a vow of chastity but it would be surprising if they never had sexual feelings. Recent revelations have shown that numerous Catholic priests and others, supposedly having chosen a life of chastity, have sexually used and abused children who were unfortunate enough to be under their control. Indeed, it seems likely that some priests and care workers chose their calling specifically to have access to children in circumstances that the general public knew nothing about. The same may have applied to some social workers and to school teachers who from time to time are sacked for abusing children in their institutions. A welter of abuse that has surfaced notably within the Catholic Church in Ireland and North America has produced a raft of recriminations, lawsuits and, in a handful of cases, the unfrocking and imprisonment of those responsible. In the UK the Criminal Records Bureau has undoubtedly made children safer from paedophilia though it has no influence upon paedophilia in the home which is still prevalent.

Ordinary people have different positions along the sexual dimension. This is partly determined by their age, with men and women having the highest sexuality from their late teens to the mid 30s. The tailing off of sexuality with age is variable. Silvio Berlusconi, the former Italian prime-minister, is 76 at the time of writing yet has been open about his need for sex with pretty women on a regular basis. As a nation, some Italians express disgust at his choice of women including girls who are barely of the age of consent or who may be prostitutes, but many quietly admire his overt virility. Mr Berlusconi, we may assume, has a position a long way from the origin along the sexual axis.

Everyone is somewhere along the economic axis because without food and basic material things we die. Self-made millionaires, I assume, must be far along the economic axis, for why do many go on piling up wealth when all their physical needs are amply satisfied? The widely accepted answer is that *power over people and things* is pleasurable in itself to economic man. It has been said the power is the ultimate aphrodisiac and examples can be seen of footballers and unprepossessing millionaires with trophy girl-friends on their arms.

Some readers may criticise my analysing mankind on just three dimensions. Perhaps it is a simplification, but all analysis attempts to bring order, and hence understanding, from information that otherwise is complex and unmanageable.

Are the three dimensions truly at right-angles to each other?
Here is a simple test which by which you can see whether my three dimensions are a useful way of analysing humans and their behaviour. Think of yourself. Have you ever been in love, or

sexually aroused, or both at the same time? Most of us have experienced those states. At those times, did your position on the spiritual and economic dimensions change? For example, did you decide that you no longer needed to work at your job? Did you suddenly, without influence from your lover, desire to go to an art exhibition or a classical concert of the sort that previously bored you?

When you are in love, many of your feelings about the world are heightened. Yet if from experience you can say that you stayed with your job and did not suddenly yearn to go to an exhibition or the Proms, you are demonstrating to yourself that the three dimensions or axes are a valid form of analysis. The essential feature of dimensions is that you can change position on any one of them while remaining stationary on the other two, as in the example you have just tried on yourself.

The three dimensions are a useful means of analysing individuals. Can it be applied to groups of individuals by nation or ethnicity? Within the western world today, from observation ordained priests of whatever religion are likely to be less economic and more spiritual than others. However, it was not always so. In the Middle Ages the Christian church was a pathway to political power, economic wealth and, possibly, to Eros. Even today, senior prelates in the Christian hierarchies enjoy a standard of living above average and have some political power as well. In Iran, being an ayatollah brings with it huge political and economic power.

Within nations or societies certain groups of people are self-evidently farther along one of the three dimensions. For example, investment bankers are enormously well paid for gambling in obscure securities using other people's money, and as a cohort they are clearly far along the economic dimension. Is it possible for complete nations to be in different positions with respect to the three dimensions? Anyone who has been to Japan and sensed the work-ethic at first hand may notice a difference when visiting Europe or, more so, Africa. I conclude that the Japanese as a nation are further along the economic dimension than the nationals of the various African countries I have been to.

From observation it is apparent that just as all individuals are at different points along the three dimensions, so groups of people — nations and ethnic groups — may similarly be at different points on the dimensions. This being so, systems of classification such as mine are both legitimate and useful for comparative analysis. Further, if individuals can change, so too can groups of people.

Are the three attributes of equal importance in determining man's behaviour? Observation and history make it clear that by far the most important dimension both in individuals and in groups when it comes to determining actions is *economic* man. *Sexual* man and *spiritual* man trail far behind.

The reasons for this are clear. Since earliest days man has been concerned with survival. Survival meant hunting game, which often was scarce, fighting for and defending territorial rights and providing for a mate and family. Economic man is concerned with survival. Following Darwin, economic man survived, so the human race to this day inherits the influence which places most of it far along the economic dimension.

47

Today economic man's goals focus upon land and energy. As an individual he has a hierarchy of needs: food, clothing, shelter and warmth are the first four. There follow a multiplicity of goods and services which he can obtain for money. He seeks land — or more generally territorial rights — for the resources it contains and the security it brings. He seeks energy as the means of transforming materials from the land into goods. Later, when his primary needs have been satisfied, he requires services such as a gardener who saves his time and energy. Economic man's aim is that he should satisfy his economic wants in the least possible time and with the least expenditure of his own personal energy.

In considering the three dimensions of man, it is important to recognise *that none of the three is an antithesis to the others*. Economic man is *not* the antithesis of spiritual man nor is sexual man the antithesis of spiritual man. If they were antitheses they would be different extremes of the same dimension rather than at right angles to each other as shown in the figure above. So, a highly spiritual man may be highly sexual or not at all, or he may be highly economic or not at all.

A word needs to be said about motivation. Motivation is not a further dimension but rather an attribute which occurs in all the other three. The approximate position of a person on each of the three axes is set by what he inherits genetically or otherwise at birth. Motivation determines where he ends up on each axis in relation to his potential.Thus a person may be born with the aptitude to become a millionaire but may never bother to find paid employment. Another with ordinary intellectual gifts may write a best-selling book by having more persistence than other people. The early submissions of

J K Rowling and Frederick Forsyth were rejected by various publishers.

Many arguments have taken place about the relative importance of nature and nurture in determining individuals' achievement. The arguments are essentially sterile unless motivation is taken into account. Observation shows that two children from a given family, brought up in the same way, can have different aptitudes and achievements. Motivation frequently explains the difference between aptitude and achievement.

Few would deny that there are clear differences between individuals however measured. However, some argue dogmatically that there are no inherent differences between ethnic groups. I find this surprising. World class sprinters of both sexes and heavy-weight boxing champions are commonly black. If there are clear, visible physical differences between ethnic groups, it follows that non-physical differences between ethnic groups are equally possible.

In this book I am primarily concerned with economic man and the economic behaviour of nations. I shall concentrate on differences in the economic behaviour of people and nations. But what of the other two dimensions? Are there differences in the sexual behaviour of nations? Observation shows that there are different perceptions of what is acceptable or not on the sexual dimension in different countries. Contraception and abortion are illegal in the Republic of Ireland. Since the country is a democracy and has adopted the laws concerned, it must be assumed that the Irish as a nation are on a different position on the sexual axis compared with, say the British. Ireland's banning of contraception implies that sex should be for producing children rather than an expression of affection or a means of physical pleasure. The Irish therefore seemingly can be placed closer to the origin of the sexual dimension than the British.

It is apparent that there are differences between nations on the spiritual dimension as well. From observation, Iranians, Saudis and other nationalities in which Islamic fundamentalism is strong are conspicuously intolerant in religious matters when compared with other nations. If religious intolerance is part of the spiritual dimension — and I am uncertain whether religious intolerance is close to the origin or far from it — at least religious *differences* are clearly observable. Religious intolerance is neither economic nor sexual so I conclude that organized religion of whatever form is part of the spiritual dimension. I suggest that different quantities of religiosity demonstrate differences between nations on the spiritual dimension.

In conclusion, I suggest that not only individuals but also groups of people including nations have economic, spiritual and sexual characteristics in differing proportions and therefore are at different points on the three dimensions. If you deny this you are forced into arguing that all nations are at identical positions on all three dimensions. This does not seem to be true. However, for the remainder of this book I propose generally to leave aside the question of differences between individuals and nations on the spiritual and sexual dimensions in order to focus on their differences on the economic dimension.

As noted, my starting point is that most people are economic most of the time. Of course there are notable exceptions. I know and admire people who have deliberately chosen a simple, non-acquisitive lifestyle but they are a small minority. Even spiritual leaders seem to be well out along the economic dimension. The Catholic Church has amassed vast riches over the ages and shows no sign of wishing to divest its wealth. Jesus of Nazareth, who told his disciples that if they had two coats, they should give one to the poor, might have had difficulty in recognising modern popes sumptuously installed in the Vatican as his direct disciples today. More recently, new religious sects such as Scientology and the Moonies have amassed huge wealth. Saudi Arabia, the possessor of Mecca and the epicentre of Islam, is preoccupied with wealth.

Are any nations *not* preoccupied with wealth? Anthropologists and sociologists may point to a few tribes, generally located in places such as the Amazon rain forests, whose members are content with a simple existence and where all possessions are shared for the common good. The paucity of counter-examples reinforces my thesis *that most people and most nations are economic most of the time.*

If you disagree with this, then put this book back on the shelf. Or, better still, read it to the end so that you can find ways of disputing the analysis it contains.

7   SEXUAL MAN

As explained in the previous chapter, this book is not directly concerned with the sexual dimension of man. The purpose of this chapter is to highlight ways in which this dimension differs from the other two.

It might be thought that sexuality was part of the spiritual and economic dimensions. The proof that this is not so is simple. It is quite possible to have sex without any of the emotions that are part of spiritual man. It is equally possible to have sex without any economic implications. Therefore sexuality in man is a dimension in its own right.

Most men and women enjoy sex at some stage of their lives. Much is currently written in the west about sex, though at other times the subject was taboo and still is so in some countries. Self-evidently there are no absolute standards. What is accepted as normal in one country or society may be considered abhorrent in others. For example, female genital mutilation (FMG) which causes immense pain and mutilates women's labia and clitoris, sexually their most sensitive parts, is widely practised in the countries of west, central and east Africa. FMG is carried out without anaesthetic, frequently causes severe side-effects, and has no purpose other than supposedly to ensure women's virginity before marriage by removing their desire for sex. The fact that it also denies them sexual pleasure for the rest of their lives and in addition can cause serious difficulty in child-birth does not seem to outweigh, in those primitive nations, the importance attached by males to having a virgin, albeit a severely mutilated one, to deflower on their wedding night.

53

Sexual activity has historically been a chosen subject for guidance by religions and, to a lesser extent, by philosophies. The Catholic Church today continues to reject contraception irrespective of the poverty and hardship caused by untenable population growth in many developing countries. The spread of Aids may have persuaded the Catholic hierarchy that condoms should be used in communities where the risk of catching Aids is high. Islam permits men to have several wives concurrently while most western societies, by relaxing divorce laws, have made it easy for men and women to have several spouses sequentially. Gay sex is now widely acceptable in the west but is punishably by death by stoning in Iran and some West African communities.

Though heterosexual relationships still predominate in western societies, homosexual and lesbian relationships have become public and acceptable. For several years in the UK, gay couples have been able to register civil partnerships which are marriages in all but name. Same-sex couples can adopt children.

Christian churches are still in a bitter internal debate about homosexuality, though the tide is clearly running in favour of complete equality for same-sex unions. The fact that the debate has occurred at all might suggest some relationship between the spiritual and sexual dimensions in man.

The relationship between sexual and other forms of motivation has been the subject of extensive writing. Freud believed the sexual urge to be the prime motive force in males though not, apparently, in females. Freud was clearly wrong. Sex may sometimes dominate actions but only when other needs have been satisfied. At one time duelling between men over a woman's honour was known, and punch-ups in pubs are the modern equivalent. However, such fights have been negligible in frequency and magnitude compared with wars about land. Two world wars and numerous minor wars since 1945 have left many millions dead on battlefields, in cities and in concentration camps for reasons totally unconnected with sex. It is obvious that the continuing efforts of economic man in his daily work are to put food on the table and a roof over his head before the needs of sexual man have even been considered. Freud had sex on the brain, which is the wrong place to have it.

Sexually, men and women are as different as their bodies. In sexual matters man is simplistic and aggressive. The reasons are clearly historical. Men with stronger bodies were better suited to hunting and fighting. Women's role, which entailed bearing and bringing up children, working in fields and tending the home, was passive and reflective. These circumstances applied in societies accounting for the largest part of the world's population. Still today in rural societies such as Africa, women till the fields but this reflects the traditional domination of men over women rather than freely chosen roles.

In the west, women rightly believe that in occupations that are not dependent on muscles they should have opportunities equal to men. This belief is strongest in societies in which the harnessing of natural (as opposed to human) energy has removed the need for muscular strength in many jobs. Thus, the women's rights movement started in the USA, a society in which natural energy has been widely harnessed to replace human energy. The more backward the society, the more manual work still entails hard physical effort and the more women are subjugated to males. Afghanistan is a case in point.

Under the Taliban, girls are denied education and women wear burkas. In Saudi Arabia they are not allowed to drive cars. In Iran sex outside marriage results in the female being lashed or stoned to death while male rapists are seldom punished. Where Islamic fundamentalists take control, as happened briefly in north Mali in 2012, women are required to wear the veil, a symbol of their historic role of subservience to men and concealment in the harem.

In western societies Roman Catholicism attempts to influence the role of women by forbidding women to use contraception or to have abortions. However, the moral influence of the Catholic Church generally is in sharp decline owing to widespread paedophilia scandals and a belief that in banning contraception and abortion successive popes have been out of touch with society.

In advanced societies the harnessing of nature's energy has greatly assisted women's liberation and will continue to do so. The fact that a few women mine coal in the USA is due to the use of powerful machinery needing skill to operate instead of brute force. In general, the more a country has learned to consume natural energy intensively, the more likely are its women to be liberated. Women have been admitted to the military in western jurisdictions though front-line combat is still not sanctioned.

Women's historical subjugation is attributable not just to their weaker physical build. Observation suggests that women are more spiritual than men. A simple head-count in Christian church services confirms this. The predominance of women in churches freely open to both sexes reflects the characteristics and inclinations of those who come to worship.

By contrast, Moslem mosques are for men only. They simply reflect Islam's historical role in enforcing the domination of men over women.

Women are more chaste than men. Some men need to relate sex to love but many men do not. For this reason female prostitutes abound while gigolos are few. Male prostitutes known as rent-boys, an increasing phenomenon in some parts of the world, serve other men, not women.

Further proof of men's higher sexuality than women's is seen in the gay communities of both genders. In gay areas of certain western cities, bars and clubs specialising in male homosexuals abound, while those that specialise in serving lesbians are rare. Head-counts at gay rallies show more gay men than gay women.

Research into the frequency and promiscuity of gay men further demonstrates that men are more sexually motivated than women. Before Aids became a threat to gay men, they could have sex at will without fear of side-effects. For women, sexual liberation occurred, if briefly, with the advent of the contraceptive pill. Thus, for about 10 years in the 1970s both men and women could have unlimited sexual encounters without, it seemed, physical repercussions. Fear of the major side-effect, an unwanted pregnancy, was removed by the Pill which also permitted more sexual pleasure to the woman than internal female contraceptive appliances, her traditional way of avoiding pregnancy. Scientists have developed other techniques to avoid pregnancy including contraceptive implants under the skin of the arm that give protection for up to three years and contraceptive injections that last for 2-3 months. A morning-after pill is another means of avoiding pregnancy. The Family Planning Association's website cites 15 different forms of contraception.

Gay men also had their own sexual revolution. As homosexuality between consenting adults became legal in developed countries many gays gratefully came out of their closets. Thus, in the swinging 'sixties and 'seventies both men and women in most western countries became sexually free to do what they wanted when they wanted. For the first time in history equality of opportunity was made available to men and women, straight and gay alike.

If sexual man and sexual woman were equally placed on the sexual dimension then supply and demand in the area of sexual intercourse would be in balance. Yet the oldest profession did not disappear in those swinging times. Today the supply of prostitutes remains considerable. Indeed the word 'prostitute' is always taken to mean a woman. Some countries such as the Netherlands, Germany and Australia have legalised brothels. In the UK the law permits performing sexual services for money but not pimping or living off the earnings of a prostitute. The police raid brothels when local people complain about them and, even more so, if they believe that the working girls have been trafficked from abroad and are working under duress.

Simply put, more men want sex, or men want more sex, than women. It is arithmetically obvious that if women wanting casual sex were equal in number to the men wanting it, if both sides wanted it with equal frequency and there were means of enabling all concerned to meet, the world's oldest profession would have to present itself *en masse* to retraining centres to learn new skills.

In fact the Internet has become the new medium for helping to balance the sexual needs of men and women, both in the paid sector (prostitution) and the unpaid sector where no money is exchanged. Websites for prostitution such at Punternet provide names, telephones and the detailed services provided by working girls together with reports on visits written by clients. Other sites exist for men and women who seek confidential, no-strings sexual relationships. There has been an effect on traditional brothels, sometimes also referred to as saunas. Some have closed and others are struggling not least because of the bleak economic climate over the past five years. Websites are replacing the traditional cards stuck up in telephone booths. In Germany it is reported that working girls have been offering big discounts to keep their clients coming.

In Sweden, however, the law imposes penalties on the clients rather than the girls and this too has influenced the amount of traffic. Studies have suggested that the number of prostitutes in Sweden has fallen since the 1990s. Studies have also shown that in Sweden there are fewer prostitutes in relation to population compared with other Scandinavian countries. It is tempting to suggest that this also reflects a traditionally easy-going attitude to sex among Swedish women generally.

The evidence seems strong that women are less sexually-driven than men. Men are interested in what women wear or don't wear. By contrast, many women appear indifferent to men's clothing and appearance. All the many top-shelf magazines depicting women with little or nothing on are expressly for men. By contrast, erotic magazines selling expressly to women can only be found by surfing the Internet. Pictures of nude men are not a staple content.

Magazines of nude men are for gays.

Women's magazines on the other hand contain pictures of fully clothed women. Fashionable women's clothes may please men but evidently they please women more so. Most women are pleased to dress well. Many women dress well to please themselves. A few women dress well to please men.

Yet further evidence of man's higher sexuality compared with woman's is found in the history of Aids. Originally this was thought to be a 'gay plague' because the first people diagnosed with it were gay males. The rapid spread of Aids in cities such as San Francisco was the result of gay men's high level of promiscuity. In Africa where homosexuality among men has to be hidden from society but heterosexual promiscuity is a way of life, women have the Aids virus in comparable numbers to men. Tribal women accept sex from men, whether it gives them pleasure or not, because in Africa man is master and women obey.

It is impossible to escape the conclusion that women are less sexual than men, while observation also suggests that they are more spiritual. It is therefore remarkable that in some major world religions they may not become priests. The religions concerned are dominated by men for historical reasons. Men, being more economic and less spiritual than women, fear to give up power over others in general and over women in particular. Women, being more spiritual and less economic are reluctant to exert pressure to enter the priesthood. However, they achieved this milestone change in the Church of England in 1992. It is hard to imagine a similar movement by veiled women in Saudi Arabia and other Islamic nations. A few brave Saudi women are campaigning to be allowed to drive.

It seems that the world would be a better place if governed by women with their higher spiritual values. The Roman Catholic Church aligns itself with Islam against women becoming priests. Catholic priests may not marry and should, in theory, be celibate as well. This opens the door for them to abuse children who are frequently available as altar boys.

Man's sexual nature ensures that the world's population will increase. Women's less sexual nature serves to limit the increase but only in societies where women are not subordinate to men and have access to contraception. The relentless increase in population is seen in sub-Saharan Africa. Only war, contraception, famine, natural disasters or disease will prevent severe overpopulation by 2050. We are already being constantly reminded that millions — perhaps one eighth of the world's population — already are permanently hungry.

Western economic man's preference for family planning will always be far outweighed by sexual man's lust which runs without constraint or contraception in Africa, south Asia and Latin America. China and India have introduced one-child-per-family policies with limited success and the world's population continues to grow much faster than increases of food-stock.

Meanwhile, epidemics have far less effect on world population than in the previous centuries. SARS, bird 'flu and swine 'flu arrive from nowhere, account for some hundreds of deaths world-wide and peter out. In the 1990s it was thought that Aids would decimate populations in Africa but treatments these days can prolong the lives of people with Aids. Population growth in Africa continues relentlessly. Over-population coinciding with climate change seems certain to alter the long-term ability of planet Earth to sustain itself and to avoid famine. Changing rain patterns, floods and droughts as recently experienced in Africa, Australia, Bangladesh, the USA and Europe will add to the problems of feeding mouths in developing countries in future. Meanwhile Africa in particular continues to produce babies while the land available to feed them is constant or diminishes. Sexual man must take his share of the blame for population growth.

8 CAPITAL AND CURRENT ENERGY

Energy is the basis of all activity. To survive, man needs energy. Food gives him internal energy. For hundreds of years fossil fuels have provided man's primary source of external energy, particularly when it has been converted into electricity or heat.

Economic man has generally made some attempts to use energy efficiently not because he was conscious of the finite nature of fossil fuel, but for short-term, practical reasons. Children leave lights on and parents turn them off because they have to pay the bills.

In other ways economic man has sought to restrict the loss of energy as heat. Friction produces heat which is dissipated to atmosphere and which makes any machine less efficient. Thus, every machine has oil or grease to reduce friction in the moving parts. The shape of aircraft and cars is designed to reduce air resistance. Air friction warmed up Concorde's body when the plane was flying at twice the speed of sound.

Energy is found in two forms. I call them *capital* and *current*. I believe this classification is original and useful for analysis. Capital energy is stored energy. Coal, oil and gas are the commonest forms of capital energy. Uranium for nuclear power is a less common form of capital energy. A lake, whether natural or man-made, also represents stored, capital energy if the flow of water from the lake can be converted by turbines into electricity.

Capital energy has the general characteristic that by itself it does not dissipate. Action by man is needed to release the stored energy.

Often this action takes the form of starting a chain reaction. Man's discovery of fire was the first example of a chain reaction that unlocked a store of capital energy. When primitive man rubbed two bits of wood together it produced friction and heat. After a bit the heat produced a spark and thence a flame to ignite the flammable gas from the wood. The burning wood produced more heat which in turn made adjacent pieces of wood hot and set them alight. Thus the chain reaction continued until all adjacent flammable material was burnt: the *capital* energy had been dissipated into *current* energy, namely heat, and all that remained was non-flammable residue.

Fossil fuels namely oil, gas and coal, which represent the bulk of man's available capital energy, are substances that nature has prepared without assistance from man. Other forms of capital fossil energy are oil-shale and lignite. They have a lower energy content than oil, coal and gas, and are more difficult to extract, transport and harness for useful purposes. For this reason much less use has been made of them. Economic man naturally prefers to exploit the forms of capital energy that have the highest energy content.

Another form of natural, capital energy is water. A lake, river or even the sea, from which hydro-power can be taken, all represent a source of energy that nature renews by the world's rain system. Hydro-power can be converted into electricity and hence, ultimately, into heat which is dissipated.

Water flowing through a dam's sluices and wind passing a mill's vanes represent a flow of current energy. Harnessing this energy was common in past centuries when water-mills and wind-mills were used to grind corn. Thus, nature's current energy in the form of wind and water power enabled another form of capital energy, corn, to be converted into current energy, food, in the form of flour.

Current energy is energy being used. Food, electricity, petrol, oil, gas and compressed air driving a pneumatic drill are forms of current energy as they are being used.

Capital energy on the other hand can generally be used as fast or as slowly as man wants. It can be switched on or off at will. Capital energy is like savings in a bank. Converting it to current energy is like withdrawing savings and using them. The analogy can be taken further. Everyone knows how difficult it is to build up savings in a bank and how easy it is to spend them. Man has become skilled at transforming capital energy into current energy but remains unskilled in his ability to store energy.

Indeed, the storage of energy is generally difficult. Before the discovery of natural gas, men made gas from coal which then had to be stored in large steel gasometers. These are still used to store man-made gas. Nature thoughtfully stores oil, gas and coal in vast underground reserves indefinitely and without dissipation or deterioration. When man tries to store energy he meets major technical problems. Electricity is the most convenient form of current energy and yet it is the hardest to store.

The simplest example is a torch battery. This contains chemicals which react to produce electric current when a circuit is made by switching the torch on. The energy in the battery remains there as a potential force for a long time. However, once the torch is switched on the capital energy dissipates as current energy producing light and heat within the bulb. After a bit, the chemical process is complete, the electrical current ceases, the bulb fades and there is no more capital or current energy. In some cases, like car batteries, the process can be reversed. Electric current is transmitted through the battery, which becomes a store of capital energy again.

In discovering that wood burns, man found the first source of capital energy that he could control. The heat was used for cooking and for making simple things such as pottery. Later he discovered that fire enabled iron and bronze to be extracted from ore and to be fashioned into implements. These implements, notably knives and axes, enabled him to cut wood more easily than with flint and so increased his ability to convert capital energy into current energy.

With the discovery of fire, nature's capital energy was used entirely as heat. Then, many thousands of years later, came the discovery of steam power. It enabled heat's energy to be transformed into mechanical energy which replaced that of man and allowed him to do countless things hitherto undreamt of. In factories a central steam engine provided motive power via pulleys and belts throughout the building. Steam locomotion was still a prime motive force on the railways up to the 1950s.

The discovery of electricity as a source of both light and energy was the next major advance which increased man's need for primary energy. Electricity was a much more efficient form of lighting than oil or gas. Converted into power by electric motors, it soon proved far more convenient than steam. It could be distributed easily by cable throughout the factory, eliminating the need for complex mechanical drive-shafts and pulleys. It could be switched on and off instantaneously unlike a steam engine which needed an hour or two to fire up and to raise steam. As electric motors became more efficient, smaller and cheaper they were built into a multitude of domestic appliances: vacuum cleaners, washing machines, refrigerators, fans, central heating pumps, dishwashers and even shavers and tooth-brushes.

In parallel with the development of electricity came the internal combustion engine. This invention became possible by the discovery of how to process crude oil which is difficult and dirty to burn, into petrol and other forms of fuel that are highly flammable. The internal combustion engine takes petrol, diesel fuel or gas, mixes them with air and ignites them in an enclosed chamber. The resulting combustion produces hot, rapidly expanding gas that forces the piston down the cylinder and then is vented to atmosphere through a valve. Thus heat is converted into mechanical energy.

One of the first and still most important applications of the internal combustion engine was the horseless carriage. In 100 years this developed into the immensely sophisticated product of design and engineering that constitutes the modern motorcar.

Within jet engines the same principle applies, namely igniting fuel to produce heat, the expansion of gas and hence mechanical energy, but the expanded air escapes directly to atmosphere instead of via a piston. However, for uses ranging from the petrol driven lawn-mower through to massive earth moving equipment, the piston-based reciprocating engine remains the most common way of transforming capital energy in the form of petrol into controllable current energy.

In the 20th century, petrol and electricity replaced steam as the prime mover of machines and vehicles other than steam engines on the railways. Indeed, the only significant remaining use of steam as an intermediate source of motive energy today is in steam turbines which generate electricity. In these, the prime source of energy, which is either fossil fuel or nuclear, creates heat which in turn vaporises water into steam. The steam passes turbine blades like wind passing the windmill, and turns them. The movement of the rotor drives a dynamo which produces electricity.

All three major discoveries, steam power, electricity and the internal combustion engine, enabled new uses for energy to be developed. By increasing demand for current energy, they increased consumption of capital energy. Countries such as Switzerland and Canada which are endowed with suitable rivers and lakes, built hydro-power systems which initially supplied the bulk of their energy needs. Most countries however mined coal. Those with plentiful supplies developed their industries rapidly and became wealthy. Those without coal, which included the Arabian Gulf states, remained poor and backward.

The importance of oil and gas as sources of primary energy was recognised early in the 20th century, but it was only in the 1950s that world-wide exploration became a central preoccupation of developed and developing countries alike. The developed countries had quickly realised that oil and gas were far cheaper to mine and distribute than coal. Oil and gas literally spouted from the ground under their own force and, being liquid or gaseous, could be pumped down pipelines or into tankers. This was much easier than sending men and machines deep into the earth to mine coal or even obtaining it by open cast mining.

The role of coal as a general prime mover of trains was largely eliminated in the 1950s. Instead it was used in electricity generating stations sited close to the mine heads. Electricity, refined oil and gas became the prime sources of mechanical energy and they remain so today. Coal-fired generating stations remain a source of domestic and industrial heating. Coal also has an important function in furnaces for making steel but is no longer a prime mover of machines.

The discovery of how to transform nature's capital energy into current mechanical energy brought new wealth in the form of abundant goods which could be made in increasing quantities and with decreasing personal effort. Man no longer had to saw timber. A machine did it for him. He no longer had to build roads with pick and shovel. Instead he operated the controls of bulldozers.

A characteristic of economic man is that he is never satisfied. However wealthy he becomes, there remain yet further goods and services to be acquired. The poor want to become rich. The rich want to become richer. Both are united in their desire for cheap natural energy to provide the riches they seek. Economic man's aims are self-reinforcing. The more he seeks to become rich, the greater his incentive to find new sources of capital energy and ways of converting them into current energy.

In the late 1950s people began to calculate when the known reserves of the main fossil fuels — coal, oil and gas — would run out but the amount of the world's reserves was not known then. This still is true.

What was certain was that the most obviously accessible reserves had been identified and that future reserves would be harder to obtain. They would be off-shore or in unfriendly parts of world such as the Antarctic and possibly thousands of metres under the sea.

Then came a new source of energy. The devastating power of nuclear energy had been demonstrated at Hiroshima and Nagasaki, and it seemed obvious to try to harness nuclear energy so that this new source of power could be available when fossil fuel began to run low. In the 1950s the nuclear energy programme began in earnest. It was stimulated when it became clear that major sources of oil and gas in the Arabian Gulf could be controlled by a handful of sheiks and that unstable regimes such as such those of Iraq, Iran and Libya could cut off supplies overnight.

The problems of harnessing nuclear energy are well known. First, the technology and fuel of power stations is broadly the same as for bombs. Countries with nuclear power stations can be expected to make nuclear bombs as well.

Second, if a nuclear power station malfunctions, the radiation and nuclear contamination are devastating. The Chernobyl disaster of 1986 has been matched by the Fukushima earthquake and sunami of March 2011 that devastated one of Japan's most important atomic energy centres. At the time of writing the fuel rods have not yet been brought under control and the possibility of a meltdown of the entire complex remains grave. For reasons of national pride the Russians were unwilling to reveal how close Chernobyl came to a complete meltdown and similarly the Japanese have been prone to understate Fukushima's dangerous future. In terms of the seriousness of risk,

Fukushima was finally brought up to level 7, the highest risk.

Many western industrialised countries have significant nuclear electricity generating plants. They now have to re-think whether to build a new generation of nuclear plants or join an unseemly dash for gas with the carbon emissions entailed and the potential impact on climate change.

Before Fukushima, politicians had a further interest in promoting nuclear power as it reduces dependence on oil and gas from unstable states, notably in the Middle East, and Russia. Now nuclear power stations are questioned even more critically than before. Large safety margins will need to be built into their construction. This will take time and money and there is a strong likelihood that gaps will appear in the future when there will not be enough generating capacity to meet peak demand. Tariffs will need to be increased dramatically to dampen down peak demand. Rationing or power cuts are likely. All these will be politically unpopular and politicians would much prefer to have plenty of nuclear capacity on hand to avoid shortages of supply. Fukushima may have taken that option away. More and more emphasis will be put on renewable sources of energy but it is most doubtful whether they will be able to produce enough output.

Spent nuclear fuel remains highly radioactive for hundreds of years and its disposal is a serious problem. Using the ocean as a bin for such waste is unacceptable. Land sites that can be contaminated in perpetuity by storing radioactive waste are not plentiful. Some spent nuclear fuel can be reprocessed and on the face of it such recycling is most desirable. However, on technical and financial grounds, it is still uncertain whether reprocessing nuclear waste will prove viable.

Finally, the world's resources of uranium, the basic fuel of nuclear power, are tiny. At best they might provide part of the world's energy needs for a few decades.

The world's capital energy was not created by man. Nature made it and stored it over millions of years. Man will exhaust reserves of oil and gas first, very likely in 60 years from now during the second half of the 21st century. Coal will last longer, perhaps another 200 years but the impact of carbon emissions on climate change looks daunting. Economic man is living off capital energy like a young man squandering an inherited fortune. Living off capital is legitimate for individuals only if they are near death and have no successors. Economic man is acting as though he is near death and without successors.

Belatedly scientists are now being required by politicians to seek how to harness hitherto neglected forms of current energy found in nature — sun, wind, waves and geothermal heat from the earth's interior. Such current energy is proving difficult to harness and to store and the resources being used to this end are still puny compared with those used to seek out new reserves of oil and gas.

The use of capital energy from fossil fuel could become much less needed if we could harness nature's abundant current energy. The world's most viable inland hydro-power schemes are already in place but tidal and wave power have barely begun to be exploited. Solar power, wind power and geothermal heat all offer prospects of clean energy when the technologies have been improved.

The powering of aircraft will present particular problems. Aero-engines increasingly try to maximise fuel efficiency, and substitute fuels are being developed for the internal combustion engine. For example, industrial alcohol refined from sugar cane is already used to power a large number of cars in Brazil.

Whatever solutions are ultimately found, one thing is clear. Economic man must stop basing the world's economy on the use of natural fossil fuel and must look on the remaining reserves as a bridging loan while we find ways to become self-sufficient in current natural energy. If we fail to develop natural energy, we shall be driven back on nuclear energy. Murphy's Law says that if something can go wrong, it will. The more nuclear power stations that are built, the greater the certainty that one or more will melt down. Further, there will be greater risk of enriched uranium being used by rogue regimes such as Iran and North Korea. This is particularly true of power stations that are maintained by poorly trained technicians in third world countries. If the USA, Russia and Japan, three of the world's most technologically advanced nations, have each experienced a near melt-down, how much more easily will such a disaster occur in Iran, India or Pakistan? And the more the world relies on nuclear power stations, the more quantities of bomb-making material will abound.

A nuclear world means living on the brink of self-annihilation. The only secure future — and one which is inevitable in the long term because of the shortage of uranium — lies in increasing reliance on nature's current energy.

Ian Senior: *Time and Energy*

9 HEAT, LIGHT, MECHANICAL ENERGY AND THE SUN

The three forms of natural energy are: mechanical power, heat and light. They are related, sometimes obviously so. For example, an electric bulb is designed to give light but also produces heat, while an electric fire is designed to give heat but also produces light. An internal combustion engine and an electric motor are designed to give mechanical power but also give off heat.

From the point of view of economic man, there is a hierarchy of natural primary energy: heat, light and mechanical energy, in that order. To survive, man needs all three forms of natural energy. Without heat he would die. Without light, his activity would be restricted to day-light hours. Without mechanical energy he would revert to a primitive life-style.

Heat
The sun is the main source of heat and potentially a source of mechanical energy. The only other form of natural heat is the hot interior of Planet Earth below its crust. Heat from either source is difficult to convert into mechanical energy. In the case of the sun it has to be focussed through lenses to obtain sufficiently high temperatures. Alternatively its heat can be captured using solar panels or photovoltaic cells. The former captures solar energy to heat water. The latter convert solar energy directly into electricity. The conversion of geophysical heat into mechanical energy presents formidable technical problems.

Light

Light is far less obviously a source of mechanical energy but ultra light-weight prototype wheeled vehicles and even very light aircraft have been powered by solar cells. All these are still far from being commercially viable products. Commercial electricity for some years has been generated from the sun's rays in a French power station and commercial solar power stations are coming on stream in Spain and the USA. Their output is predicted to provide only a small part of national needs.

Natural mechanical energy occurs as a result of heat and light. Rain, which produces mechanical energy in rivers, results from the existence of the sun. The growth of vegetable matter, which produces combustible biomass, also results from the existence of the sun.

Two forms of natural mechanical energy do not stem from the sun. They are tidal energy for which the moon is responsible; and mechanical energy from natural geysers which shoot water into the air, sometimes at predictable intervals. Tidal movements are predictable and dams can be used to harness the water flowing between high and low tide, but their construction coupled with side-effects on the area have so far made barrages commercially unattractive.

As noted, heat and light are closely related. The atomic particles of a conductor — generally a form of metal — are excited by electric current so that they produce electro-magnetic radiation in the form of heat and light in varying quantities. At some frequencies light is given off. At higher frequencies the radiation becomes invisible to the human eye. At certain frequencies this electro-magnetic radiation is used for telecommunication, broadcasting and the remote control of domestic appliances.

The transformation that has taken place in the application of electricity over the past 50 years has been extraordinary. Initially, electricity's role was that of providing heat, light and mechanical energy. This role remains, but to it has been added the dramatic world of information technology in which the role of electricity and electromagnetic radiation is to carry information between humans and machines and within machines themselves. In this context, the role of electrical current is solely to communicate information. Any heat that is generated is undesirable, so the higher the conductivity of the circuits the better.

Heat and light can be measured. At one extreme scientists have found that a complete absence of heat — and hence light — is minus 273.15 degrees Celsius. There is no theoretical limit to extreme heat. Water boils at 100 degrees Celsius at sea level but it boils at lower temperatures as the atmosphere becomes thinner, for example halfway up Everest. Steam can be raised to far higher temperatures under pressure and this is the principle of steam locomotion. A furnace fired by oxygen is less hot than the sun. The heat at the centre of an atomic blast is comparable to the heat of the sun's centre.

An interesting scientific development over the past 20 years has been the development of new techniques for observing heat which is invisible to the human eye. As children we learn that some things, notably fire, that give off light also give off heat and should not be touched. Yet many people have burned a finger touching a hot iron or a saucepan. Scientists have found that by using infrared photography, objects can be recorded according to the heat they give off. This technology has practical applications such as discovering how best to insulate buildings. Using satellites, the world can be photographed in infrared to give information about climate, vegetation and crops. Inevitably there are also less attractive military applications. Missiles are guided to their targets by the heat which these give off. People can be identified in the dark by their heat and so can be shot at.

The close relationship between heat and light is elementary to a scientist but in the context of the present book it has a more profound significance. *Heat and mechanical energy are the analogue of economic man. Light is the analogue of spiritual man.*

Heat, light and mechanical energy combine to generate output. When man exerts effort, he produces mechanical energy and becomes hot. When he dies, his body is no longer capable of mechanical energy, loses its natural heat and becomes cold. Every process that is used to transform materials into finished products requires a combination of heat, light and mechanical energy. As noted earlier, mechanical energy is often a transformation of heat. In general, without heat or mechanical energy for which electricity is a standard source of power, very little can be transformed. The growth of vegetation requires heat and light though not mechanical energy.

I use the words "very little". What are the exceptions? Chemical reactions including fermentation transform the materials concerned. These can take place without heat, electricity or mechanical energy. Grape-juice turns into wine spontaneously. However, even making wine entails bringing together or separating the ingredients and so requires mechanical energy.

Physical reactions normally release heat. Friction in any mechanism entails the dissipation of energy in the form of heat. Electrical circuitry dissipates heat when current flows through it. Economic man's existence is entirely concerned with transforming raw materials in ways that they can be used and, in some cases, consumed. Cooking is the most elemental example of this. Most foodstuffs can be eaten raw but applying heat makes them more appetising or easier to chew and digest.

As with an electric fire, the energy in food can be measured. The commonest units of measurement are kilocalories (popularly abbreviated to 'calories'), joules and watts. All goods and services, like food, are the end product of heat and mechanical energy used in some way. Economic man devises ways to use energy to make or do the things he wants.

Light is the second principal manifestation of energy. As a rule applications of light need much less primary energy than heat. For example, a 100 watt bulb can light a room. The same room may need a 2000 watt fire to heat it.

The three main human senses concerned with communication require light or mechanical energy. Sight requires light. Hearing requires sound which is mechanical energy in the air. Touch is another form of mechanical energy.

The human voice was the earliest form of communication and

remains the primary medium for communication at a simple level. If I receive a simple instruction, hearing it is enough. If it is complicated, I must write it down. Writing and reading require light as the medium of communication between the page, the eye and the brain. The ability to speak and write has differentiated man from all other animals. Even sound, the second most important medium of communication, is a manifestation of energy. Sound is produced by mechanical energy which vibrates via air or some other medium. Sound cannot travel through a vacuum.

Touch is a lower level of communication but still requires mechanical energy. A blind person reading Braille does so by the motion of his finger tips over the page.

Every aspect of modern civilisation requires light as a medium of transmitting and storing knowledge. Imagine how man would adapt if one day everyone became blind. Braille, as form of transmitting and storing knowledge, is infinitely clumsier than the written word and technical drawings. It is clear that without light or sight, civilisation as we know it would revert, literally, to the dark ages. Similarly, without heat, civilisation on the earth would perish within months or weeks.

Light is energy used for information and communication. In early days beacons gave warnings. Lighthouses and the flashing lights on police cars and ambulances still do so. It is remarkable that today, in an entirely new way, light has become the medium of the information technology revolution. Until recently, electric current was the dominant medium of telecommunication. Telephony consisted of an electric current that carried an analogy of the human voice. Today light, transmitted along tiny fibre-optic cables, is rapidly replacing copper cables and electricity as the main medium of telecommunication.

Light is higher up the radio spectrum than other radio frequencies and therefore can carry vastly more information. The most important advance in telecommunication, equivalent to the development of the transistor as an electronic switch, was the development of fibre-optic cables that canalise light and can take it round corners. The information that can be contained in each fibre-optic path is many thousand times greater than could be carried by traditional copper wires and uses much less energy. Thus science has begun to yield the most desirable of results: more information transmitted yet requiring less electricity (current energy) and less copper wire and switching equipment (capitalised energy).

When light is intensified or concentrated, its energy content can be harnessed. As children we learned to use a magnifying glass to concentrate the sun's rays on to a dry leaf and make it burn. Lasers have become a technology of a new generation of office printers and are also used in surgery to replace the scalpel. It is clear that through major advances in the processing of radio magnetic waves — fibre-optics, microwaves and lasers — light is becoming the pre-eminent medium of information and communication, supplanting physical energy in the form of electricity and catching up with the world's oldest form of communication, sound.

Just as heat and mechanical energy are the analogue of economic man, light is the analogue of spiritual man. Light is a central theme in many religions. Generally it is equated with goodness while absence of light, or darkness, is equated with evil. This is seen in Christianity. In the Bible, wise men followed a star. Jesus is referred to by the gospel writers as light and Satan as darkness. These examples draw together the concept of light as an amalgam of information and of goodness. The word "lighten" means to make less heavy, "enlighten" means to inform; "illuminate" means to cast physical light and also to make comprehensible. Thus our language recognises the relationship between light, information and understanding.

A further relationship between light and spiritual man is found in Raymond Moody's *Life after life*[7]. This remarkable book gives case accounts of people who have been declared clinically dead for short periods but who have revived. They are able to describe the act of dying. A common feature of these case histories is that the dying person finds himself outside his body. He can see his body, the room and the people in it. Then comes a sensation of travelling through a dark restricting tunnel at the end of which he encounters a bright light. This light is intense yet not blinding or painful. The light communicates with the person in a way that is kind but profoundly questioning. In most cases the person who has died does not wish to return to his body but does so because of some unfinished activity in his life.

Life after life, like the case histories of hypnotic regression given earlier, is immensely impressive. There are evident parallels between Moody's description of dying and Christian teaching about passing through the valley of the shadow of death. Equally important is the

---

[7]   Moody J R *Life after life*, Bantam books, 1975

relationship between spiritual man, wisdom and light. If man has a spirit that is non-physical and therefore is not extinguished at death, that spirit, by definition, is not based in or dependent on physical energy as we know it. Nor, it seems, is it bounded by the dimension of time as we know it.

The sun

For planet Earth the sun is the physical synthesis of heat and light, that is to say of energy in its two primary forms. The sun is also an analogue of time. As far as mankind is concerned, the sun will last for millions of years and is predictable. For this reason since earliest days the sun has been used to measure time. Days and years derive from Earth's relationship with the sun. The moon, which reflects the sun's light, gives us months. Astronomers have noted that sunspots are not predictable and may influence seasons and the weather. However, the general nature of the sun is predictable.

Most of economic man's activity is geared to the sun. He works during the day and sleeps at night. Most animals have a cycle that is also geared to the sun and to the seasons. Primitive man who had no means of artificial light except fire was largely dependent upon the sun. Modern man with electric lighting can work or sleep when he pleases but a preference for being awake during the day and sleeping at night is still well established.

The sun is the prime source of the world's energy. Without its heat and light all life on earth would cease. Vegetation would stop growing, water would freeze and mankind would be extinguished in a matter of months at most. We take for granted that this will never happen, but in doing so we prefer to forget that there were ice ages.

We do not know what caused them but they could return. The balance of the natural environment which has produced sophisticated life on earth is fragile. Even in the past five hundred years it is possible to note significant climate changes. For example, it is many years since an ox was roasted on a frozen river Thames. Scientists need to be able to explain and predict such changes in the climate because all life still depends on the sun.

Much interest is now being taken in the "greenhouse effect" in which it is claimed that man, by burning fossil fuel, is both heating up the atmosphere and, because of certain gases, destroying the earth's protective ozone layer. Both have the effect of heating up the earth. This in turn will melt the Polar regions, raise sea levels, flood large areas of land and dramatically change the face of the earth. If this were to happen, it remains true that man's activity in releasing heat into the atmosphere still remains very small by comparison with the daily quantity of heat provided by the sun.

In addition to providing direct energy to keep us warm, the sun provides other forms of indirect energy. Food grows and vegetation renews itself. The sun vaporises water into rain which later becomes the power for hydro-electricity. The sun's heat causes movement of wind, a further form of current energy. Small wonder that the sun, the single and total embodiment of the world's light and life, was worshipped by past civilisations. We may not now worship the sun in a literal sense but we should continually give thanks for its existence.

The energy of the sun's heat on earth is vast and represents far more current energy than we consume from other sources. Unfortunately it is difficult to capture because it is so dispersed. As noted, solar panels are now used to provide domestic hot water and a number of systems are available which use photo-electric cells to convert the sun's energy into electricity. These cells provide power to astronauts in space.

So far the amount of mechanical energy or heat produced by all these systems together has been insignificant. Instead, man in his wisdom has continued to rely on fossil fuels. Even the harnessing of wind and water has been more common that harnessing the sun.

The sun is not only the source of most current energy but also of capital energy too. Coal, oil and gas all are the fossilised work of the sun over countless millennia. Unfortunately, there is no prospect of the sun kindly repeating its production of fossil fuels in our lifetime!

Much more importantly, the sun is a source of safe energy. Coal, oil and gas when burned produce carbon pollutants which collect in the ozone and then damage the environment. The dangers of nuclear fuel are so appalling that most people prefer to ignore them altogether and to leave decisions on nuclear power stations to politicians and scientists. However, the green movement is growing in strength and in Germany, for example, has obtained a measure of political power. The decision by the German government, following the Fukushima catastrophe, to stop building new nuclear power stations is hugely significant. It will make Germany dependent on electricity imported from France which is increasing its nuclear building programme. The UK is dithering about replacing its ageing nuclear power stations. Forecasts show that we have already run out of time to avoid shortfalls in domestic supply. Only EDF, a French company, is still showing interest in building new nuclear stations in the UK and other potential suppliers have dropped out of contention. Fracking is now being considered as an interim source of natural gas, but the process is still questionable in relation to the long term pollution of water tables and increasing carbon emissions.

Only one thing is certain. The sun will continue to provide energy in the form of heat and light and will do so even if shining on a barren planet in which life and vegetation have been destroyed by a wayward creature, economic man.

10 CREATION AND FORGETTING

Economic man creates ideas in his mind and transforms materials into finished goods. The motivation for creating ideas usually comes from his needs. For example, man disliked carrying heavy things so when he saw that tree trunks could be used to roll heavy objects he invented the wheel. Necessity was and is the mother of invention.

Today much is invented that could not by any stretch of the imagination be described as necessity. A new brand of soft drink could not be described as a necessity when many brands already exist, but for the company striving to survive, a new flavour, even just new packaging, may make the difference between profit or loss, survival or insolvency. From the viewpoint of companies, invention is still necessary for survival.

Most acts of creation are motivated largely or entirely by economic man. Far fewer are motivated by spiritual man alone. A person may feel moved to write a poem without any expectation that it will be published, still less paid for. Many people paint as a hobby with no expectation of selling their pictures. However, a number of the world's greatest creators were at their most productive because of the demands of economic man in them. Mozart composed and Balzac wrote prodigiously to keep creditors at bay.

It is important to distinguish between *creating* and *transforming*. People sometimes use the term "creating" loosely as in "creating a dress". The act of creating comes in conceiving a new design in the mind. The production of the dress itself is the transformation of existing materials. Transformation requires skill and energy.

Three tests can be used to define *creation* and *creativity*.

1   Creation requires little or sometimes no energy. By contrast turning a creation into a finished product always requires energy.

Man creates when he composes a tune or writes a novel. Creation comes from the mind, not the hands. The composer hears the tune in his mind. He does not require additional energy to create the tune though he does require energy in recording or executing his creation. He clears his mind of competing thoughts and addresses himself to creating a tune which he then writes down. This may require a pencil, a keyboard or a computer. If he clears his mind and mentally sings a nursery rhyme he is not creating but remembering. Whether he is creating or remembering his body continues to function at the same rate, consuming the same amount of energy. The execution of some creations may take much energy, for example executing a sculpture or erecting a building, but the original creation has occurred before execution takes place.

2   A creation can be used or played indefinitely yet remains complete

A tune can be played a million times yet it remains the same tune. A picture can be looked at or copied a million times but remains the same picture. By contrast a chocolate bar can never be a creation since it can be consumed only once.

3   A creation cannot be destroyed

Creation and destruction are generally held to be opposites in language. In the context of this book they are not so. *The opposite of creating is forgetting.*

You cannot destroy a tune but you can forget it. Dictators can order certain music not to be played and can have the records or printed versions destroyed, but they cannot order music to be forgotten. If there is accurate memory the tune can be transcribed anew and played again a million times after the dictator is gone. In practice, memory is imperfect so original works of art such as pictures, buildings, sculptures, plays, poems and music can be "destroyed" by being physically destroyed and then forgotten. Even if they are remembered after physical destruction, it is difficult to recreate them perfectly. Yet the fundamental truth remains that only the materials or the medium have been destroyed. The original creation can be reproduced perfectly if there is perfect recollection.

Ideas, philosophies and religions, like works of art, are created in men's minds. As creations they cannot be destroyed, only forgotten. That is why they are potentially such powerful forces for good or evil. They can be spread almost effortlessly by word of mouth, in writing, or by any of the modern media. Beliefs, truths, half-truths and lies can influence one man or a million with little additional expenditure of energy. If I play a catchy new tune on television the next day a million people can whistle it. If the television sets were switched on anyway, the additional energy cost is zero.

Because the cost of all forms of communication continues to fall dramatically, the possibilities for propagating new ideas or new creations in whatever field are becoming increasingly extensive. Social media on the Internet such as Facebook and Twitter appear to be costless at the point of use. In practice, they are paid for by advertising which in turn must be paid for by sales of goods and services. However, once a text message has been uploaded to a social network, there is no additional cost to the sender or the recipient. The systems become a modern form of broadcasting. Similarly a BBC broadcast costs the same amount whether it is heard by one million or a thousand.

In parallel to the very low and falling cost of transmission, the means of recording, transcribing and storing creations are becoming more sophisticated and dramatically cheaper all the time. Vast encyclopaedias and hundreds of full length films and television programmes can be stored on small hard-drives or if preferred they can be stored on central servers and accessed on demand. This means that there is now no need to have a library of CDs and DVDs at home. The quality of high definition and three dimensional broadcasting has enhanced the value of the programmes stored centrally compared with traditional DVDs held at home. The bandwidths available for broadcasting digital transmissions are sufficient to support hundreds of channels up to the point at which saturation is setting in.

That said, the media are *not* creation. The medium is *not* the message. Cheaper, easier media may bring forth more creations in volume terms. They enable people to create who in earlier times might not have done so and they may increase the creativity of creative people. Shakespeare today, seated at a word-processor or a recording machine, might have doubled his output of plays. However, it does not follow that a doubling in the number of word-processors will double the number of Shakespeares.

Man differs from animals in his ability to create. Animals' creative

Ian Senior: *Time and Energy*

ability is limited. Ants have created the concept of heaps and bees of hives. These are extremely complex by the standards of most other creatures, but they are trivial in comparison with a dishwasher.

91

Ian Senior: *Time and Energy*

11 TRANSFORMATION AND CONSUMPTION

All people at all times are transforming or consuming or doing both simultaneously in different proportions. The concept of consuming is well understood in what is often termed the consumer society. Transforming is a concept that generally is less accurately described as 'producing' or 'processing'.

Economic man *creates* without using incremental energy. When he processes or transforms he uses incremental energy. Nature, by organic growth, produces vegetation in all forms. The earth is endowed with organic and inorganic matter of innumerable forms. Economic man *transforms* them into finished goods which he then consumes. Economic man produces nothing other than babies. Every economic activity of man in relation to materials is *transformation*.

When people are at rest, they consume little but not nothing. Consider a man living on a desert island with coconuts. When he is asleep on the beach he is not transforming but his bodily processes are at work digesting the coconut he ate for lunch. By contrast, when he awakes and eats a coconut he is consuming in a more obvious way. Finally, when he carves a coconut shell into a bowl he is transforming it.

In an industrial society man consumes even when asleep. In his kitchen his fridge is still consuming electricity and the electric clock on the wall keeps ticking consuming energy from the batteries inside. More importantly in terms of energy consumption, the central heating or air-conditioning may be on. In his sleeping state man consumes little natural or personal energy but the moment he awakes he begins to consume both rapidly. He switches on lights, heating and the cooker, drives to work in a car and operates a bulldozer for eight hours. The bulldozer driver at work has consumed a vast amount of primary energy, petrol, but has created nothing. Instead he has *transformed* a piece of land into a motorway. After work he drives home again, turns on lights and heating, cooks a meal and switches on the television.

Throughout the cycle of a working man's day, he is consuming some personal energy and, in terms of calories, vastly more natural energy. Even an office worker, as opposed to a bulldozer driver, consumes large quantities of natural energy by commuting to work and occupying a heated building with lights, lifts and a large variety of electrically operated equipment.

To gain an immediate feeling for the difference in the amount of personal energy a man consumes compared with natural energy, think of the last time you tried to push a car with a flat battery to get it started. Two or three strong men pushing an average car on a level road strain their utmost to get it moving at five miles an hour. The petrol engine with one litre of petrol will move the same car at 70 miles an hour for ten miles or so. Man's personal energy is puny compared with that of natural energy.

All transformation of materials requires energy and conversely it is impossible to transform materials without using energy. Even chain reactions such as fire or other chemical processes require energy at the outset. Thereafter the chain reaction may provide its own energy. When chemical agents are brought together they react without further human intervention: for example acid with zinc. However, the transformation of raw materials into acid and zinc requires energy as does bringing them into contact with each other.

The transformation of goods requires energy and so do all services. Traditional services, for example that of a gardener, are intensive of human energy but have become less so. A musician who performs at a concert is providing a service. Even the triangle player in the orchestra must use *some* energy to give his performance.

When a creation is consumed it is in no way diminished or destroyed. When a good or service is consumed it is partly or completely destroyed. No one else can eat the piece of chocolate I have just consumed. Similarly, if I spend the night in a hotel room I have "consumed" that service and no one else can have it. By contrast, when a plumber mends my tap I have consumed his energy but not his skill. Skills are the result of training the mind to co-ordinate the body. As such, skills are like creations: they cannot be destroyed, only forgotten.

Some goods seem to be usable without being consumed, but in practice all wear out. Each time an axe strikes wood the axe becomes blunter because some metal is lost. A few goods are purely decorative. Strictly speaking they are not used and therefore need never wear out. Consider a diamond set in a ring. The gold setting may wear out by friction from the finger, but the diamond, as the saying goes, is forever. The paradox however can be resolved. Economic man consumes goods and services literally. Spiritual man takes his satisfaction from the senses, particularly sight and sound, without having to consume. Economic man may possess an old master painting, regarding it as a form of investment which at some stage may be exchanged for consumable goods. Spiritual man will not be concerned with its monetary value but only with its aesthetic value to him. Economic woman looks on a diamond as store of value — a girl's best friend. Spiritual woman looks on it as a thing of beauty or of commitment from the giver.

The following statements show the difference between transformation and consumption, which can be thought of as two opposite ends of a spectrum:

- transformation requires the input of personal time and energy. Consumption often requires little of either;

- economic man prefers to consume rather than transform;

- consumption is generally pleasant. Transformation may be unpleasant if it requires physical effort;

- transformation entails net expenditure of personal energy. Consumption generally entails a net gain of personal energy.

12 WORK AND LEISURE, PAIN AND PLEASURE

For periods of economic man's life, notably childhood, education and old age, he only consumes. As a minimum he eats food, wears out clothes and needs a roof over his head with heating to keep him warm. During his working life western man may work or transform for seven hours a day for 235 days a year for 45 years. This gives 74,000 hours worked per working person's life. The number of hours in a life of 80 years is 24 x 365 x 80 = 700,800 hours. So, if everyone worked full time for 45 years from 20 to 65 they would work for just 10.6 per cent of their lifetime's hours.

Clearly not every individual in a society works 74,000 hours. Some members of the potential workforce including the disabled are unwillingly unemployed and some are willingly unemployed having chosen not to work. Therefore the number of hours actually worked on average falls by say 12.5 per cent of the potential working hours. This reduces the number of hours actually worked by the potential labour force to 87.5 per cent of the 74,000 hours per working person. The average hours worked falls to 64,750 hours. This is 9.2 per cent of the hours in a lifetime.

We now have the remarkable result that in the present industrialised world the efforts of individuals while at work have to support themselves while not at work (e.g sleeping, on holiday or in retirement) and all the individuals who are not in work at all for whatever reason. The latter may be asleep, studying, sick, disabled, retired, unwillingly unemployed or willingly unemployed such as housewives or house husbands. In essence, because of the availability of cheap natural energy, economic man in industrialised societies has learned how to live in unprecedented comfort by applying just 9.2 per cent of his lifetime to providing services or transforming materials for the entire society of which he is a member.

In backward economies, notably in Africa, South America and much of the Indian sub-continent, the proportion of time spent working is higher for a number of reasons because the life-span is shorter by many years. Further, the quantum of man-hours and personal energy needed to obtain a given product, say one kilo of wheat, is higher since the planting and reaping are done by hand instead of by machine.

Work and leisure
The concept of work is well understood but less easy to define. In the first place one person's work is another person's consumption. If I bake bread and sell it, that is my work. If I bake bread to eat at home, that is my housework and in practical terms it does not count as work when the output of the economy is measured. If I bake bread simply because I enjoy doing so and eat it at home, that could be described as my leisure rather than work.

For clarity I define work as *transforming materials or providing a service whether for sale on the open market or not.* This definition includes home-based activities of all sorts including baking bread. Housewives and others argue correctly that if they had to pay someone do the household chores the value of their work would be officially recognised and measured.

This debate, though interesting for measuring national output, is unimportant in the present context. Work, for the purpose of the present analysis, is the transformation of materials or the provision of services. Both of these consume human energy and take time.

In an industrial economy, when a person works, he generally wishes to exchange the output of his work for other goods or services. A labourer digs a ditch in exchange for money which in turn he exchanges for food and other needs. A houseperson cooks for the family in exchange for having a dwelling to live in and money to buy the food. The point which is common to both activities is that they take up time and energy of the person concerned.

The motivation for work of whatever sort is varied. Some people dislike their work and do it only because they want to be able to exchange their output for goods or services which they could not otherwise obtain. Some people enjoy their work and continue past normal retirement age even when they already have all possessions and the life-style they want. Such people are the minority. In essence, there is a spectrum from those who love their work passionately and those who hate it vehemently. Most people lie somewhere on the spectrum between wanting to work all the time and not wanting to work at all. We would like more leisure (ideally with the same income) but few people of normal working age would wish to be entirely without work and to experience a low standard of living. Work then for most people has some negative connotations. They see work as something in which they give their time and energy in exchange for a wage. Many, perhaps most, believe that their time and energy should be minimised to produce a given output and a given wage, or, alternatively, their wage should be maximised for a given input of time and energy.

The amount of time which people spend at their work is one key measurement by which they are paid. The hourly or monthly rate is determined by the labour market and the value of the individual to the organisation. In the industrialised world a small proportion of workers are paid piecework rates for the number of items they produce, say shoes. A number of the professions are paid by the hour, for example lawyers, physiotherapists and sex workers.

In the simplest case the worker exchanges his labour for money only. He exchanges personal time and energy for cash. His first need is food to replace the energy he has spent at work and to keep him alive during the non-working periods. Food is energy, and like all forms of energy it can be measured in (kilo)calories. If a man uses more calories working than he receives in a currency exchangeable for food, he dies. In subsistence farming the crop is not exchanged for cash but is consumed directly. If the crop's calorific value is less than the calories needed to keep the worker and his dependants fed, they starve to death.

In even the poorest economies, most workers exchange some goods and services using money. If a farmer has a surplus of food after his dependants and he have been fed, he exchanges the surplus for money or for other goods and services. Money is the medium that enables such exchanges to take place conveniently. Barter is another means of exchange but a much less useful one.

The more backward the economy, the more work entails physical energy. Historically, in every land peasants tilled the soil by hand, aided by beasts of burden. Even in the industrialised west, horse drawn-ploughs with labourers trudging behind them were found in the 1930s and '40s.

Because physical labour is often uncomfortable, particularly in bad weather, workers sought ways to reduce the discomfort. Farmers bought tractors rather than trudge behind the horse. Through the industrial revolution of the 19th century onwards, factory workers sought shorter hours. However, the replacement of physical labour by machines in factories was often resisted. In those days unemployment meant serious deprivation and possible starvation. Many workers preferred appalling conditions of work without machines to the prospect of fewer jobs with machines and unemployment for the rest.

Historically work was mainly physical, and physical work was often uncomfortable or painful. Accounts of working on farms, in factories and down mines in the nineteenth century are plentiful. By current standards the conditions were unthinkable. Thus historically there has been a strong relationship between work and discomfort or even pain. Only in the past 50 years or so and only in the world's industrialised economies has that relationship all but disappeared. Today some people such as fishermen on trawlers and deep-sea divers on oil rigs face severe working conditions, but everywhere in the west conditions have improved. Most outdoor jobs entail far less physical energy than before. Historically, roads were made by navvies with picks and shovels. Today one man with a bulldozer can achieve as much as a gang of 100 navvies and in much less time.

Leisure has always been pleasant particularly when it was the counterpart of severe physical effort. Today complete industries are devoted to enhancing yet further the enjoyment people obtain from leisure. The food industry in the west is no longer about survival but about the pleasure of eating.

Historically leisure, as respite from work, entailed using the minimum of personal energy. However, today even quite lowly paid jobs have become sedentary and leisure, by contrast, may take the form of deliberately spending considerable personal energy. People jog, play a variety of energetic games and perspire in gyms and health clubs.

The urge felt by a significant proportion of the population to work off surplus physical energy and body-fat represents a rare phenomenon in the history of the human race. The Greek civilisation was one in which bodily fitness was an end in itself. In some societies today fatness is seen as a sign of wealth and therefore to be admired. The wives of African chiefs are often fat.

Fatness is the visible symptom in industrialised societies of the excessive supply of food over demand for it. Eating today is about greed, not need. The preoccupation with slimming of people in all walks of life, particularly among women, indicates an availability of food unparalleled in the history of industrial society and requiring the minimum of effort to obtain and cook. Today in industrialised economies, we are nearing the end of the golden age for cheap food. Its cheapness derives in considerable part from cheap energy to plant, harvest and process it. We have found ways of consuming nature's resources of capital energy at a rate unparalleled in history. Materials such as steel have become easier to process and to turn into cars and washing machines. In parallel we have become cleverer at using robotic tools to replace much of the labour in the traditional manufacturing processes.

Nature's reserves of capital energy are being rapidly consumed and energy prices are increasing steadily. Manufacture, transportation, construction, food production and processing all depend on capital energy in the form of oil and gas with both of them frequently converted into electricity. New reserves of capital energy will be found but China, India and parts of South America require increasing amounts of capital energy and other natural resources to bring prosperity to their poor millions.

The future of energy hinges largely on whether nuclear energy becomes accepted as safe both during the life of power stations and after decommissioning them. If nuclear energy increases to fill the gap that will steadily be left by natural capital energy, we can look forward to having the amount of energy we need until about the end of the 21st century. But if the cost of energy, both capital energy and nuclear, continues to rise, leisure will recede correspondingly. Cheap holiday air travel will become expensive again. Big four-wheel drive, gas guzzling cars will be replaced by economical minis. Tractors will become more expensive to run as the cost of petrol substitutes rise, and food will become much more expensive. Flowerbeds will be converted into vegetable gardens.

Pain and pleasure
Pain and pleasure still have relationships with work and leisure. However, work has become less painful and some leisure activities more so, so the relationships can be blurred. Marathon runners spend time and energy doing something which is painful a lot of the time.

The consumption of goods and services provided by others is generally pleasurable. Most forms of leisure and pleasure entail consumption. Reading a book or listening to a concert are the nearest things to exceptions. An individual copy of a book borrowed from the library can be read by many people without being consumed. A concert can be listened to by an audience in one hall or broadcast world-wide without the music being consumed. Such leisure activities make modest demands on people's time and energy and on the world's energy resources.

The book, along with newspapers, is being rapidly supplanted by electronic media. In the USA e-books now have larger sales than printed. They sell at half the price or less and can be down-loaded to reading devices in a matter of minutes. Films and television broadcasts can also be downloaded. The digital revolution shows no signs of slowing down. As digital books, newspapers and films have no printing, storage, packaging or transport costs, their relative price compared with traditional media will continue to plummet. By contrast, the costs of the traditional media will increase steadily, partly because of the cost of the materials and energy needed to produce them and partly because falling circulations will mean that the overhead costs of writing the original text will have to be spread over fewer sales units.

CDs and DVDs are already a dying medium. Their replacements in the form of hard-drives can hold a thousand full length films in a container the size of a shoe box which is getting smaller all the time. They require almost no storage space in the viewer's home. Centralised digital storage is now so cheap that a system such as YouTube can continue to accept a seemingly limitless volume of uploads of audio-visual material which is accessible free to the general public.

E-books have already eaten massively into the ordinary paper-back market. Books of reference such as bulky encyclopaedias and dictionaries have been superseded by Google and the Internet. All newspapers, for which a paper-based format used to be considered a particular asset, now publish e-versions. The saving of paper is enormous and distribution costs disappear. Readers can choose the topics and articles that interest them and ignore the swathes of writing that do not

Magazines are following newspapers. Newsagents and bookshops are closing. The customer base is ageing. School children from 10 or so onwards have become a generation of mobile-phone users. All modern mobiles have access to news via the Internet. Electronic tablets give high resolution images. They will continue to displace paper-based media as a means of personal communication. Electronic social media such as Facebook, Twitter and Linkedin are becoming ephemeral broadcast media in their own right.

To the extent that the new electronic media and the digital revolution stop trees being cut down and vans transporting stacks of newspapers large parts of which don't get read, the growth of the digital age is to be welcomed as friendly to the planet and reducing demand on its capital and current energy. The side-effects in terms of pornography and violence that the Internet offers do not affect demands on the Earth's resources but may have an undesirable affect on children for which society is beginning to pay a price.

Countless leisure pursuits entail far more use of natural energy than reading a book: motor racing and tourism to name but two. The few pleasures that entail no demands on natural energy at all are purely aesthetic and spiritual — watching a sunset or listening to music, for example. Further, it seems clear that the higher an individual scores on the economic dimension, the more his pleasures make demands on natural energy. Successful business tycoons surround themselves with energy-intensive goods such as big houses, heated swimming pools, large cars and private aircraft. Spiritual people from hermits in history to Mother Theresa of Calcutta make far fewer demands on natural energy and on products that use it. Despite this, it cannot be assumed that highly spiritual people invariably economise on natural energy. Popes travel extensively and I assume that the large Vatican buildings are well heated in winter.

The historical divide between work and pain on the one hand and leisure and pleasure on the other has been blurred by an abundance of natural energy yielding an abundance of goods, services and leisure. When there is no longer an abundance of natural energy the divide will become clearer again. Cheap holiday flights will disappear and business flights will dwindle. The latter will increasingly be substituted by video-conferencing which already exists using Skype.

13 RELIGION, PHILOSOPHY AND CUSTOM

Economic man acts according to economic principles, notably material self-interest. Spiritual man is guided by other principles and beliefs. These may be derived from religion, philosophy, custom, upbringing or a mixture of all four. Distinctions between them are frequently blurred.

Religions, philosophies and customs come into being in various ways. Usually some influential person such as a king, prophet or thinker gains a following during his lifetime. His teachings or edicts are copied, sometimes written down, and become a point of reference in later years. However, as any lawyer knows, even simple words can be open to interpretation. As a result it is common for sects and sub-sects to separate themselves from the main religions, philosophies and customs, each group believing that it has more truth on its side.

The leading practitioners of most religions, philosophies and customs are often intolerant. The Troubles in Northern Ireland, the 15 year civil war in the Lebanon, the seven year war between Iran and Iraq, the wars between the former Yugoslavian states and the civil war in Syria were or are between sects of the same religion or between different religions. They continue a long line of religious wars through history from biblical days, through the crusades and onwards for several centuries in Europe.

It has been argued that such wars are not really religious but have to do with economic matters such as ownership of land. Yet the fanaticism of leaders such as the Iranian ayatollahs and Osama bin

107

Laden seem sincere enough. Leaders, whether religious or otherwise, need followers. The Iranian ayatollahs and Bin Laden's successors evidently have these in large numbers.

Philosophy can also be a profound influence on spiritual man. In this field there is more freedom for adaptation and change. Philosophers do not claim divine revelation. Their writings more commonly draw from the work of previous philosophers and thinkers whom they must first refute or upon whom they build their new beliefs.

The most influential recent philosophers have been the political economists whose theories set out how societies can or should be organised. Adam Smith and Karl Marx are two whose influence has been immense. However, their writings are generally considered by their followers not as divine truth but as building blocks from which advances can be made.

By contrast the divine truth ascribed to Christianity, Judaism and Islam has its roots in books which in turn are believed to represent truth revealed direct by the divinity to chosen prophets. Thus "truth" is held, at least by fanatics, to be immutable. Changes in the wording of the scriptures are largely ruled out and instead can more conveniently be ignored. Thus the Mosaic commandment, "thou shalt not kill" has been ignored by Jews, Christians and the protestant and catholic sects for three thousand years. Sadly, even minor changes to the interpretations of the scriptures give rise to killing and to unspeakable cruelty by sect against sect. Who could think it matters whether bread at Christian communion transubstantiates into the "body of Christ", a Roman Catholic belief? Points such as this have separated Christians for centuries and gave rise to the Inquisition, assassinations, torture and burnings at the stake in the name of a religion within which a central commandment was and is "thou shalt not kill". Similarly the mutual hatred and the wars between Shi'ite and Sunni Muslims date back to who should be the true successor to Mohammed when he died in 632 AD.

The role of political philosophies, notably Marxism, socialism, and fascism, have also been justification for abhorrent acts of cruelty against others: the gulags in Russia under Stalin, the holocaust under Hitler, the Cultural Revolution under Mao Zedong and the massacres in Cambodia under Pol Pot are glaring examples.

Customs are more nebulous than religions in their origin and are more adaptable. In the past they may have derived from monarchs and the nobility. The way of pronouncing the S in Castilian Spanish is said to have been in respectful imitation of a queen with a lisp. However a particular custom originates, it is seldom universal and is subject these days to increasingly quick changes of taste and fashion. The length of skirts is one example.

Customs deriving directly from religious teaching are sometimes contradictory. Strict Hindus eat no meat while less strict Hindus eat meat but not beef. Jews and Muslims do not eat pork, and certain parts of some animals are regarded as inedible in one society and a delicacy in another. Sheep's eyes are prized in Arab cuisine, frogs' legs in France, tripe in parts of England and haggis in Scotland. Horse meat is sold as standard by some French butchers but is regarded as distasteful in the UK. Dogs are eaten in the Philippines. Foreigners are likely to find these forms of meat unpalatable but only if they know what they are eating. Customs may change at times from new learning or scientific discovery. The relationship between smoking and lung cancer has widely reduced the amount of smoking as a social skill in western society.

Spiritual man is the focus of a vast range of tenets deriving from religion, philosophy and custom. He is taught some beliefs and customs as part of his upbringing and education; others he absorbs in childhood from his surroundings. Later as an adolescent or adult he questions what he has been taught and either finds it acceptable or begins a quest for truths, standards, philosophies or customs that satisfy him. In doing so he may find himself in conflict with economic man both within himself and outside. His chosen religion may tell him that material goods are to be shunned. Economic man tells him that they are pleasurable and an essential prerequisite to comfort and security.

Upbringing is probably the most potent force in determining spiritual man's concept of life. Observation shows clearly that people born into Muslim societies are likely to become Muslims, people born of Christian parents to become Christian and so on. However, the advent of the mass media has made it easier for new customs, religions and outlooks to become fashionable rapidly. These may be as trivial as hair lengths or as obnoxious as drug taking.

The established religions have not been immune to changes that are possible in the new era of mass communication. The ordination of women in the Church of England began in 1994 and the ordination of women bishops has only temporarily been thwarted by a minority of traditionalists in the Anglican community. Catholic priests' celibacy has been relaxed in the case of married clergy who convert to Roman

Catholicism. Gay marriage has been legalised in some western states. Twenty years ago these developments would have seemed out of question.

Faced with such tidal flows in thought, religious leaders are vulnerable and insecure. The written word which for centuries was largely unchallenged no longer provides answers to current questions. Reinterpretation is one answer. Was Jesus really the son of God, was he born from a virgin and did he rise from the dead? A former Anglican bishop of Durham had doubts on doctrines such as these.

To reinterpret scriptures, whether the Bible, Torah or Koran, is to threaten the edifice on which the religion is built. If reinterpretation is considered to be legitimate and valid, then for hundreds of years everyone else has been wrong. If it is possible to reinterpret now, it will be equally possible to reinterpret next year too. Absolute truth gives way to relative truth, to half truths and ultimately perhaps to no truth at all. Successive popes, seeing the danger of this progression, have stuck resolutely to established dogma and to belief in the pope's infallibility when speaking on religious matters *ex cathedra*.

The foregoing analysis shows the inherent vulnerability of any religion or philosophy today. It is particularly vulnerable if it was set down centuries ago in different circumstances by people writing in different languages or not writing at all. Yet spiritual man is a reality. His belief in a God or gods over centuries does not seem to be pure hallucination. The unfortunate intolerance of spiritual man towards those who hold different beliefs is the strongest indictment of religion, philosophy and custom as a guide to personal behaviour.

To say that there is no full understanding of God or gods does not prove their non-existence any more than does an imperfect understanding of stars or the behaviour of atomic particles. However, it is noteworthy that in most religions spiritual man ascribes to the deities the two absolutes which he himself does not have: limitless time in the form of immortality; and limitless energy referred to as omnipotence.

14 THE THEORY OF TIME, ENERGY AND HUMAN BEHAVIOUR

The theory set out in this chapter is concerned only with economic man. I recognise that actions of spiritual man and sexual man are also factors in human behaviour. However, my fundamental thesis is this:

Most people are economic most of the time.

Further, I suggest that economic man remains more predictable than spiritual man. This justifies basing my interpretation of the past and present and my perceptions of the future upon the actions of economic rather than spiritual or sexual man.

We have seen so far how the concepts of time and energy are central to the analysis of economic man. Before defining the theory let me first summarise some fundamental yet obvious truths.

To survive, every man must receive no less personal energy than he expends. Food is energy in its most fundamental form. Economic man is a reservoir of energy just as a lake is a reservoir of water. If a reservoir gives out more water than flows in, it becomes empty. Similarly, if a man expends more physical energy than he takes in as food, he dies. The amount of energy that each person needs to consume as food depends on his lifestyle but a typical male's metabolism burns off about 2000 kilocalories per day. Women, who are lighter, burn off less energy and so need less to eat.

In a warm climate, if a man has food and water he needs nothing else for survival. In a cold climate he also needs clothing and shelter. Thereafter he has no more absolute needs though there are still limitless goods and services he would like to have as well.

Every article that economic man wishes to possess represents *capitalised* energy. A coconut on a tree represents capitalised natural energy. A man who picks it from the ground has spent no personal energy in obtaining this particular natural store of energy. A car, on the other hand, represents a mass of capitalised natural energy and a much smaller amount of capitalised human energy. Natural energy in various forms and enormous quantities has been used to mine ore, produce steel and fabricate a finished vehicle. By comparison, only a little human energy has been used at each stage from mining the ore to assembling the components on the production line.

The coconut is natural capitalised energy, namely biomass created by the chemical reactions of a tree, rain and sun. The car is the outcome of the application of nature's fossil energy to minerals. Every product of nature or man consists of capitalised energy. The entire economic system consists of trading energy, either as capital energy or as current energy. Goods that are bought and sold represent trading in capitalised energy.

The labour market consists of trading human time and, to a much lesser extent, human energy. At a simple level, a value is set on the speed at which people work aided by machines. A typist whose speed is 50 words a minute should earn more than one with only 30 words a minute. A photocopier that produces 50 copies a minute commands more value than one that produces 25.

Economic man continually trades his personal time and energy for energy in other forms. If he remains a subsistence farmer with his own plot, he exchanges his time and energy for food energy from his plot. If he has a surplus of food he exchanges it for goods or services supplied by others. For centuries economists and other thinkers have started from the simplified assumption that industrial economies are concerned with the production and exchange of goods and services. In truth, industrial economies are concerned with

- the application of natural energy to transform raw materials into finished products;

- the application of human energy to transform raw materials into finished products or to provide services;

- the exchange of products and services; and

- making claims on other people's goods and services.

Money is the means that enables exchanges or trade to take place between willing parties. Goods and services are priced in part upon the time and energy required to bring them to the market and in part upon how supply and demand fluctuate. Supply and demand are brought into balance by prices that enable markets to clear.

We have already noted that man has no energy of his own. Three fundamentals can now be stated:

1) *capital* energy enters the economic system when deposits of oil, gas and coal are discovered or an atomic power station is built;

2) *current* energy enters the economic system as food and when

oil, gas and coal are burned, atomic power is switched on and when windmills and water mills turn; and

3)   economic man constantly seeks to possess or control the largest possible quantity of capitalised or current energy either in its raw form or in the form of food, goods and services.

In order to acquire goods and services economic man uses money which is the most useful medium of exchange and much more convenient than barter. Money, as a unit of measurement, serves as a simple way that enables economic man to buy and sell goods and services and in doing so to maximise his well-being, sometimes called his "utility".

If a rational economic man is paid £10 per hour for a given job but the firm next door will pay him £11 per hour for doing the identical job in identical circumstances, he moves to the firm next door. In this way, for the same net expenditure of personal time and energy he obtains a larger claim on other people's time and energy. The difference between the personal time and energy he expends working and the time and energy he can buy from others constitutes his *net gain* of time and/or energy and determines how labour markets work.

A crucial additional factor is the set of skills that each economic man can offer in the market place. Some skills are rudimentary— for example cleaning offices— and take no time to learn. Other skills, for example those of a brain surgeon or astrophysicist, take years of education and training to acquire. Because of this their skills are in shorter supply than office cleaners and they command a much higher hourly wage.

If economic man has to choose between two jobs with the same number of hours requiring the same sets of skills and the same pay, he takes the one with the highest value in net energy. Hourly rates of pay reflect supply and demand in the skill sets concerned. If the same rate of pay for the same number of hours were offered to deep-sea divers as to office cleaners, economic man would generally choose the cleaning job. In practice deep-sea divers are paid much more than cleaning staff. Ignoring complex matters such as danger, discomfort and anti-social hours endured by deep-sea divers, we should still expect deep-sea divers to be paid more than clerical staff per hour because they expend more personal energy and must therefore receive more claims on (food) energy in order simply to remain alive.

I have discussed my concepts of time and energy in some detail. There is one other word in my theory which is easily understood: *utility*. Utility is a neutral word meaning something on which I place positive value. If I obtain food, a car, a holiday or indeed any good or service that I desire, I obtain utility. Utility is a useful concept which can embrace any of the following in varying degree:

> convenience
> comfort
> happiness
> pleasure
> satisfaction
> well-being.

Disutility is simply the opposite of utility.

I can now state my general theory as follows:

Utility = energy divided by time

This can be simply expressed using the symbols

$$U = E/T$$

where U = utility

T = time

E = energy

In the formula all three signs are positive. Time moves forward and therefore is taken to be positive. For simplicity, time can be measured in hours. Energy, meaning receipt of energy, is taken to be positive. Hence utility is positive. Under the formula, if I receive a loaf of bread for one hour's work we have the equation:

$$U = \text{(one loaf of bread) divided by (one hour.)}$$

If I can receive two loaves of bread for one hour's work, utility is increased, though not necessarily doubled. Similarly, if I receive one loaf of bread for half an hour's work, utility is increased, though not necessarily doubled. The reason why the ratios are not constant is because I may have all the bread I want, so doubling its amount hardly increases my utility if at all. However, I can then sell or exchange the surplus bread I don't want for other goods or services offered on the market.

In the formula so far E has always been positive, because I receive bread, which is capitalised energy. However, if I am *expending* energy, E becomes negative. For example, if I dig someone else's ditch for an hour U becomes negative or a disutility. So -E means inconvenience, discomfort, unhappiness, pain, dissatisfaction, lack of well-being, or giving out energy.

The functional relationship between utility, time and energy is variable from person to person and, within the same person, from one moment to another. Thus, to double the amount of E while holding T constant does not automatically double U. If I am sitting in front of a fire and the heat is doubled I may be in discomfort with reduced utility. Someone else who likes a fug might experience increased utility.

The fact that utility varies from individual to individual and within the same individual at different times does not detract from the equation in explaining how economic man is concerned at all times with increasing his utility. He does so by varying his outputs of energy or expenditure of time in relation to the changes in utility he will receive from doing so.

We can now express my theory as follows:

Economic man maximises his receipts of net energy for a given amount of his time.

An alternative way of expressing the theory is this:

Economic man minimises the time he must give to acquire a given amount of net energy.

The theory relates the two absolutes, time and energy, to utility which is the sole and permanent goal of economic man. In both forms of the theory one of the absolutes is held constant while the other is permitted to vary. In this way it can be seen how economic man trades his time against energy and his energy against time. The trade-off varies according to the preferences and skills of individuals offered in the market place.

In the remainder of this book we shall discover how the theory usefully explains economic man's quest for utility, past, present and future measured in terms of time and energy.

PART 2:
TIME AND ENERGY AS
EXPLANATIONS OF THE
PAST AND PRESENT

15 FOOD, LAND AND TRIBALISM

Food is the first essential for survival. In warm, fertile climates it is the only essential. People there can exist naked and live from wild fruit and nuts. However, in most parts of the world clothing and shelter are desirable or essential in some seasons. Inuit people need them always.

All sentient creatures consciously and actively seek food some of the time. The amount of time they spend doing so depends on the ease with which it can be found and its energy content when found. For example, cows at pasture have no trouble finding food which is all around them but spend a large proportion of their time grazing or ruminating — a further part of the digestive process — because the energy content of grass is low. A large animal like a cow must eat a large quantity of grass to sustain its body. Cows give off some energy as body heat and yet more as milk. Because food is always immediately available to them they lead a placid life with little movement. The energy balance of a mature cow consists of taking in enough energy in the form of vegetable matter to balance the output of energy needed to sustain its bodily functions including a continuing supply of milk.

Horses represent an interesting contrast. They have been domesticated as animals to ride or pull vehicles. Their traditional food also is grass but the output of energy required of them by man is in the form of physical movement, not milk. The relationship between the energy output of horses and cows can be thought of as the number of surplus calories each species produces for the benefit of man. It would be possible to take milk from a cow, convert it into butter which is highly flammable, burn it to raise steam, and use the steam power to drive a vehicle. Alternatively, and more simply, it is possible to harness the cow (or ox) to the vehicle. From man's point of view the same result would be achieved: food energy in the form of vegetable matter has been converted into mechanical energy in the form of motion. The relationship of the input of food energy to the output of mechanical energy is well known to horse owners. A horse fed on oats instead of grass becomes more energetic because of oats' higher energy content.

Early man, like all other creatures, found himself in a generally hostile environment in which survival depended on finding food. Why did man along with a large number of other creatures become carnivorous even in places where food in the form of fruit, nuts and varied forms of vegetation were available? The reason is to be found in the relationship between time and energy.

Suppose a hunter needed one hour to kill a deer and the deer yielded 20 kilos of meat. Generally, the hunter could not gather 20 kilos of fruit in one hour. Moreover the energy content from one kilo of meat far exceeds that of one kilo of fruit. Thus, by hunting, economic man obtained much more net energy in a given time. Following his hunt he was left with time for leisure pursuits such as sleeping or painting the walls of his cave.

With the elimination of much wild game the relationship between the hunter's time and energy deteriorated. Hunting might yield nothing whereas farming and animal husbandry yielded food with reasonable certainty in return for the time and energy taken to till the fields and harvest crops. Therefore, depending on the availability of game on the one hand and agricultural land on the other, economic man made choices about how much of his time and energy to devote to farming or to hunting.

Since land provided the territory for wild game or for farming, territorial rights increased in importance as populations grew and more food was needed. Economic man laid claim to land to farm or to hunt over. If others encroached on his land he fought them for it. In general, larger groups could defeat smaller ones, so families joined together into tribes. The families intermarried reinforcing physical similarities of appearance and developing a common language, culture and customs. Thus tribalism was borne out of the necessity for economic survival.

Tribalism in its original form is still extensive in numerous societies, notably in Africa, parts of South America and the Indian sub-continent. Interestingly, it has survived most strongly in warm climates. Tribalism at a different level persists in northern Europe and North America particularly where migration has taken place. For example, the Irish in the USA remain strongly nationalist.

Nationalism and the concept of the nation state are simply tribalism on a larger scale. There are the same unifying factors, notably language, custom and physical characteristics such as skin colour and facial features. Tribes and nations have generally been based on territories, and wars have almost always concerned the ownership of land. The Balkan wars of the 1990s between Serbs, Muslims and Croats were solely about land. For millennia the general rule has been that tribalism, nationalism and wars were rooted in attempts to increase ownership of land.

Territorial boundaries initially were not easy to mark but occasionally tribes or nations built boundary markers to establish their territorial rights. The remains of major walls and forts still exist. In general, natural boundaries were easiest to designate and defend, so tribes and nations sometimes chose rivers or a range of hills as natural boundaries. To this day it is still common for natural boundaries to be preferred. Israel considers the west bank of the river Jordan to be a natural boundary.

The physical and social characteristics of tribes and nations resulted initially from families grouping together for the purpose of survival. Newcomers who did not have the same characteristics were seen as a threat. They were clearly identifiable and they represented additional claims on the available resources of food and land. Thus strangers were unwelcome in general but particularly at times of economic hardship. To this day immigrants are universally unwelcome in countries where the resident population feels its standard of living to be threatened. All prosperous countries have immigration laws to control the influx of would-be economic migrants.

As tribes and nations became established, land ownership became codified in law. The Doomsday Book was an early attempt to record territorial rights across a nation. During this period hunting wild creatures became mainly a sport of the nobility. The supply of meat became the function of farming and animal husbandry. Territorial rights and wealth came to be one and the same thing. Land yielded food which then was the only known form of energy other than fire and beasts of burden. Those with land were rich, those without were poor.

Landowners who wanted to become richer and lazier hired the services of the landless to work the land for them. Society became structured on the basis of land ownership and, in some measure, still is so today.

In working the land economic man, whether landowner or not, was guided by my general theory. Each economic man sought ways to increase the net energy from his work in a given amount of time. If other people did his work for him at a suitably inferior wage, the landowner increased his utility. The concept of service industries was born.

An important discovery was that animals could be made to do the work of men. A field ploughed by an ox or horse took less time and far less human energy. Later, economic man found ways to increase the yield from a given hectare of land by crop rotation and by dung. In recent years the use of tractors and other machinery together with artificial fertilisers have massively increased the yield from land while at the same time reducing the amount of human time and energy needed for a given quantity of output. In industrial economies, even those that are self-sufficient in food, the proportion of the workforce in agriculture is typically only a few per cent.

In parallel with the steady increase in the yield of agricultural land, two factors ensured that territorial rights continually increased in importance. First, economic man, even when his basic needs had been satisfied, still wanted *more* wealth. Second, populations continued to grow. This meant that more food and space were needed. However, in most societies land ownership had become fixed at an early stage. Those with land had little incentive to sell it because they were already wealthy, while those not having land were unable to save enough by working for the landowners to buy plots, assuming that these were available. Therefore those with land remained rich; those without land remained poor and as populations grew, larger numbers of poor people had to make do with an already limited amount of land which they rented from the owners. The redistribution of land is invariably one of the first promises of revolutionary organisations in South America and Africa, for example, but it proves more difficult to accomplish than to promise.

The discovery of coal, oil and minerals had a dramatic effect upon the value of land and upon the distribution of wealth in society. Those lucky enough to own land with deposits achieved windfall wealth overnight. This wealth spilled over to many of those owning no land. For example, in the Gulf today there are several million expatriate workers who own no land but who enjoy a standard of living higher than in their home states because they are servicing the oil based economies. They support themselves and also remit funds to their families at home. Their savings may even be enough to enable them to buy land when they finally return to their home country.

The social benefits of the new wealth created by exploiting nature's reserves of capital energy have been widely recognised though often they have been thought of negatively. The industrial revolution in Britain brought mines and factories with long working hours, often in unspeakable conditions. Factory and mine owners became rich. Children worked in factories and small boys were forced to climb up and sweep inside chimneys. Nevertheless, the industrial revolution, based on the availability of cheap capital energy in the form of coal, ultimately brought manufactured goods in large volumes that became widely available.

The real booming of the consumer age began slowly between the two world wars and then accelerated in the 1960s. In that period bed-and-breakfast accommodation (B&Bs) would display signs saying H & C in all rooms, meaning a hand basin with hot and cold water. Modern B&Bs are expected to have central heating and en-suites. In the 1960s many houses had no telephone. Today the ownership of a mobile phone and a land line are standard, though the use of the latter is falling. In the 1960s car ownership was patchy. Today a primary constraint on car ownership is less about wealth and more about the problems of parking in inner cities. All these material goods, which unquestionably bring utility, have occurred because of economic man's inventiveness coupled with the availability of cheap natural energy.

A further aspect of the new wealth based on exploiting the world's capital energy is the changing status of nations' importance in world affairs. The Gulf States including Saudi Arabia which until the early 1950s were little more than a collection of date-producing sheikdoms, now command world attention because of their oil wealth. In 1990 a major though brief war took place to liberate Kuwait following Iraq's invasion *because of* Kuwait's oil. A decade earlier when Russia invaded Afghanistan no such war occurred because Afghanistan has no oil or gas. The west's invasion of Afghanistan in 2001 was based on the knowledge that the Taliban government was allowing its territory to be used for militant jihadist training which produced the infamous suicide airliner attacks on the World Trade Center's twin towers, the Pentagon and, had the fourth aircraft's mission succeeded, the White House.

The origins and aims of the allied attack on Iraq in 2003 are still widely debated. At the time, the US and British governments made their main case on their claim that Saddam Hussein still possessed chemical and biological weapons of mass destruction. As is now well known, the intelligence was faulty even at the time that it was being used as the main justification for the invasion. It was disputed by Hans Blix, head of the United Nations weapons inspectors in the run-up to the Iraq war. The invasion was not officially justified on the need to protect the west's oil interests but on the danger imposed by an Iraqi president who had used poisoned gas on his own Kurdish people in El Halabja in 1988 and who had rockets that could reach Israel. In this context the invasion had the seeming justification of self-protection from a dangerous dictator, but unquestionably there was the underlying expectation that replacing Hussein with a different regime would stabilise one of the world's major oil and gas producing regions.

In parts of the world where there was no oil and gas the fertility of the land became the criterion for warfare between ethnic groups. A continuing example today is the state of Kashmir whose ownership is disputed by India and Pakistan. It is a fertile area and attractive to tourists. As such it is coveted by two states that have chronic food shortages. In Africa, by contrast, minerals in the Democratic Republic of the Congo add huge value to land over and above its agricultural use. This explains why China is becoming an important investor in the country.

The instinct to fight for land runs deep in economic man because land historically meant survival. Even when the land was barren he instinctively fought to acquire and to defend it. The Gaza strip, the west bank of the river Jordan and the Falkland Islands are examples of poor quality land that has been fought for bitterly. Economic man's instincts to grasp and hold land, implanted in him since earliest days, will not wither in a generation or two.

16   EDUCATION, TRAINING, PROFESSIONS AND SKILLS

In the industrialised world, we take education for granted. Informal education begins in some families with educational toys and parents reading aloud to their children. Nursery school education begins for most at three or four. Formal education starts at five and carries on to sixteen or seventeen. After school, a significant proportion of pupils go to university or to vocational training which typically lasts 3-4 years. Thus 10 to 11 years of education are the norm in industrial societies and 16 years are common. In some professions such as architecture and medicine, training continues for at least three years after the first university degree. From the age of 16-22 young people start a job and normally expect to work until 60-65.

A characteristic of training and education is that is absorbs much human time and little human or natural energy. A teacher or student judges whether or not he is working hard on the basis of the number of hours he must put into teaching or studying. He expends little personal physical energy.

Because the process of learning requires time, some methods have been developed to accelerate the learning process but so far these do not appear to have replaced a significant amount of traditional teaching. School and university courses have stayed roughly the same length over the past 50 years. It is true that the fields for study and the amount of information that has to be covered have increased vastly in that time and this may suggest that the learning process has also improved. Technology has helped, most notably in the past decade in which the Internet has provided access to unlimited

133

information free at the touch of a computer's mouse or a tablet's screen.

Distance learning by computer appears to offer ways of eliminating the traditional method of teaching, namely one teacher standing in front of a group of students. The new way of learning by computer seems to be most applicable to the humanities and other soft disciplines but less to science and engineering which are the subjects that will determine the future of civilisation on planet Earth.

Personal computers continue to become smaller, more powerful and cheaper in real terms. Meanwhile the roles of mobile phones, desktops, laptops, tablets and television sets are merging. The advance of technology continues to accelerate providing ever faster wireless connections, ever increasing storage on hard drives and "cloud" technology on massively powerful central servers. Television sets continue to become larger with higher definition and three dimension effects. E-books can be downloaded in seconds and stored by the thousand. The same goes for television programmes. Since these can be stored so easily the need to watch a particular programme at a scheduled time is decreasingly necessary. Use of the traditional mouse and keyboard is being replaced by touch screen technology.

The digital age has been embraced by younger and younger children. Cheap toys for five-year-olds sometimes include a touch screen. Most school children from ten upwards have mobiles. All adults these days need mobiles and e-mail addresses and only some elderly still have avoided having a mobile telephone and a computer with an e-mail address.

For a short period vast stores of information, equivalent to the Encyclopaedia Britannica, were offered on compact discs but are now available on the Internet. The information can be updated, transmitted digitally over fibre-optic cables, stored, manipulated, converted into graphics, edited and deleted in seconds. All this means that the learning process can be improved by eliminating unproductive effort such as going in person to a library rather than sitting in front of a computer and having the library come to you.

However, it is by no means certain that the speed at which humans can absorb and retain information can be *accelerated* in any comparable way. This is because the amount of information and its complexity is advancing as fast as information technology itself. Thus, the modern doctor probably still needs his traditional six years of basic training because of the increasing knowledge base to which he has access. The memory of most humans is finite, so the modern general practitioner needs to learn how to access knowledge rather than to retain it. This applies to every profession and vocation. Computers and ultra-rapid digital transfer of images will continue to assist the hands-on functions of all the professions. For example, it will be possible for a specialist surgeon in one location to operate on a patient in another location by seeing the patient via a digital connection and moving the necessary surgical equipment by robotic remote control.

The information technology revolution results from the invention of the computer and all the peripheral equipment that these thinking machines operate. However, information technology would have been of far less significance had it not coincided with the golden age of cheap natural energy. Information technology enables economic man to spend more time thinking and less time doing. Cheap energy has the same function. Yet, without cheap energy economic man would still personally have to do the things he had thought about. For example, when the world's stock of cheap fossil fuels has waned further, a farmer with a computer will still be able to work out more efficient ways of running his farm, but tractors and the fuel to drive them will be relatively far more expensive. In due course this may bring a return of cart horses and men walking behind the plough.

Cheap natural energy and increasingly cheap information technology have both resulted in more young people going on to higher education. Thus, the increasing base of knowledge has been spread over a larger number of brains. Today a typical student's brain has heard, recorded and stored far more information than would have been the case 50 years ago. What is certain is that an educated mind, now as in the past, represents *capitalised time* in the form of learning and so is analogous to a finished manufactured product which represents *capitalised energy.*

The sale price of a finished good reflects the value of the capitalised energy required to make it including the capitalised labour costs. Similarly, the fee charged by professional people reflects the capitalised time that has gone into their education and training. If, for example, a person trains to become a solicitor and pays for the entire vocational training himself, he has made a significant investment of time in himself. When he begins to practise, he must aim to charge fees that reward the *capital investment of time* he has made in his training as well as the *current cost* of his living and professional expenses.

The contribution made by students or their parents to investing in their higher education varies considerably from country to country. In the USA and elsewhere the student or his parents make a substantial financial investment if he goes to a private school or university. If he goes to a state university, he is likely to pay less because the university receives funds from the state.

The reason why governments wish to pay for schooling is straight-forward. Uneducated people are less employable and more likely to become a drain on public resources. Thus it is in the state's interests that everyone should have good basic education. In essence, industrialised states think it worth investing taxpayers' money on school children in order to avoid spending tax-payers' money on state benefits for adults later in life. Education, from the state's point of view, does not need to be thought of in grandiose terms such as the inalienable rights of man but more simply as a rational decision in the allocation of public time and energy.

After the state has provided its young people with the basic skills of reading, writing and arithmetic, what skills does it need at higher levels? Clearly the list is extensive beginning with scientists and engineers and ranging through doctors and other health-carers, police, professional soldiers with some lawyers and accountants thrown in for good measure. In addition a steady flow of teachers of the above subjects is needed to ensure a continuing supply of qualified trainees. However, it is far from clear to what extent the state needs philosophers, anthropologists, sociologists, economists, historians, psychologists, actors, musicians, classicists and a range of other such disciplines. Some of all these professionals must be desirable in a civilised society but their numbers can and should be determined mainly by the market.

How does the state ensure that institutes of higher education are producing the right number of people with the needed skills? The systems are confusing and confused. At first glance this might be blamed on the historical autonomy of institutes of higher learning. Some of the most renowned are self-funding such as the Ivy League universities of the USA. In the UK many receive a substantial part of their funds from state grants but still retain a measure of academic autonomy in the courses they teach and the number of places they offer on each course.

However, the concept that a centralised state is all-wise in predicting future demand for particular skills and professions is wrong. The medical profession is a case in point. For decades the NHS has relied on foreign doctors and nurses coming to the UK while at times British trained medical students have found it hard to get a job in the UK. British hospitals have regularly needed to recruit doctors and nurses from abroad.

The case for requiring students at universities and vocational establishments to pay a significant part of their fees rests on two arguments. The first is that if they do so, they will be more careful in choosing their course of study. It is much easier to opt for soft courses such as the social sciences and media studies than for the sciences. In this context I use the terms 'hard' and 'soft' without judgement. By these words I mean that the information that is the body of 'hard' courses constitutes facts that are provably right or wrong. A scientific experiment that is repeated by different people at different times and in different places must produce the same 'hard' results. By contrast, historians may agree on the dates on which events took place but the rest is 'soft' interpretation. Was Richard III a good king or a bad one?

I suggest that modern societies need enough scientists and engineers to give us the prospect of conquering the ills of our time, for example environmental pollution and Aids. It has much less need of people who believe they have the last word on Richard III. It is therefore in the interests of governments to focus available public money on the 'hard' forms of training and to let the 'soft' ones be taken care of by the market. If you pay for a university course you are bound to take account of your prospects on the labour market when you have completed it.

If society needs more scientists, engineers and doctors, it makes sense for the state's resources of time and energy to be allocated accordingly. Trained scientists or engineers can, if they want, buy a book or go to evening classes to learn about Richard III, and they can readily catch up on graduates in the 'soft' disciplines. The arts qualified graduate cannot catch up with the 'hard' disciplines just by reading books. The language of science including maths is the necessary starting point. Science and engineering laboratories simply are not available to non-scientists. The two cultures, so clearly described by C P Snow, are separated by a one-way filter. Scientists and engineers can fairly easily become lawyers, sociologists, economists and historians but movement in the opposite direction is impossible.

To leave the quantity and quality of 'soft' disciplines to the market does not mean that they will disappear but rather that they should have to justify themselves. As popular television programmes prove, there is great interest in history and hence there must be a corresponding demand for historians. Museums attract visitors even if they have to pay an entrance fee. If the general public wants to enjoy history as a leisure pursuit, there need to be qualified historians to teach them. Those historians will find employment which in turn will financially justify personal investment of time and energy in their own historical education.

If students know that *their own* money is required for higher education and want the best possible return, they will make informed choices given their aptitudes, the cost of the course, and the career prospects on graduation. If, on the other hand, all courses are provided free or at the same price students will make less well informed choices. In the UK, the Blair government decided to impose fees on university students at a flat rate of £3,000 per year. This was a blunt approach. The decision by the present coalition government to allow universities to increase their tuition fees up to a maximum of £9,000 per year has introduced an element of price differentiation. One result is that some universities have decided to close particular courses and departments owing to the cost of running them and insufficient demand. A few universities have decided to offer some courses at £6,000 per year.

The charges levied by each university for each of its courses should broadly reflect the time, qualifications and hence the salaries of the tutors and the capital energy in the form of buildings and equipment that individual courses require. In theory, a mathematics or a philosophy department requires nothing more than whiteboards and felt-tips whereas the scientific and engineering departments require laboratories with expensive equipment.

In applying to university each student now has to weigh up the financial cost of the available courses at his shortlisted universities. The gross fees and living expenses charged by the universities will often by offset by means-tested bursaries. There are now several "good university" guides with details about the perceived quality of the courses at different universities and the proportion of graduates from each university who are employed/unemployed one year after graduating. As discussed later, money is a proxy for measuring the input of time and energy needed to provide a particular good or service. It seems very reasonable that students who will benefit during their working lives by the quantity and quality of their higher education should be able to make informed decisions based on the costs of the education they receive.

At the age of 18 few students have savings and instead the concept of student loans has become established. Student loans have been applied for some years in the UK and, despite predictable opposition from students, have now become an accepted way for students to co-finance their higher education.

What light does the theory of time and energy throw on the question of student loans? The time dimension at present is less important to the student since most undergraduate courses are three years. Those that last four years will seem attractive to students if the state is paying for them, for they postpone the day of entering the real world and make a living. The time dimension has increasing importance if the student must make a co-payment to each year of his course. To take a four year course he must invest one third more than for a three year course, and so he is compelled to make a rational choice on whether the additional time and energy (expressed in monetary terms) that he must spend from his own pocket can be justified in terms of the reward it will bring in terms of higher wages when he enters the labour market.

The role of government should be to ensure that public funds are used in such a way that society's needs are met most efficiently. It is not difficult for governments to know which skills are under- or over-supplied. Every institute of higher education has a service to assist placing its graduates, and their statistics show which disciplines are in demand and which are not.

At Oxford University a course in chemistry lasts four years compared with history which is three years. A rational student choosing between chemistry and history should take account of the amount of his time and money required to complete each course and the financial rewards available to him on graduation. Governments and universities' careers services can expect to have better knowledge of supply and demand in the labour market for graduates with different degrees than young people of 17. Assuming a shortage of graduate chemists and a surplus of historians, a rational government will make conditions for students on the chemistry course more attractive than for courses on history. The co-payment required for the chemistry course could be reduced by the government to below that of history. The student would then make an informed choice based on signals provided by the government's and universities' knowledge of the graduate labour market.

When working correctly, a labour market is an expression of the way in which employees sell their time and energy to employers at a rate that enables the market to clear. Clearly vocational influences are also at work. A chemistry graduate might choose to become ordained and thus earn a reduced salary, but vocational influences are generated by spiritual man. The choice of employment is largely the preserve of economic man.

In summary, higher education represents an investment of time and energy by the student in himself. Students expect to get a return on their investment during their subsequent career. The state spends taxpayers' money on higher education and it has a duty to do so wisely and economically. Permitting or encouraging different levels of tuition fees for disciplines that are needed, as opposed to those that are not, is logical and wise.

Ian Senior: *Time and Energy*

17   TRADE AND CHOICE OF OCCUPATION

Man has always been concerned first and foremost with survival. In some parts of the world, notably Africa and North Korea, millions still starve, many of them to death. One of the most pressing problems is to find ways not just to prevent starvation but to raise food production in Africa above subsistence level. In the industrialised west mechanised farming has raised food production to the point when in some years there are big surpluses.

The tragedy that many have been quick to notice is that these surpluses cannot be bought by the countries with food shortages because they have little or nothing to offer in exchange. The west must give the food away free or not ship it at all. Clearly relief of immediate starvation is the first priority but handing out free food is no long term solution because it undercuts local farmers and encourages the dependency culture. Most people in developed and developing countries alike agree that trade is better than aid. Why is this?

Trade is the exchange of goods and services. When two people trade freely they both feel better off. Trade between nations is the same but the transactions occur between companies rather than individuals. When all the transactions are summed both nations are better off. There has been an increase in utility on both sides.

Socialist nations have sometimes tried a different form of trade in which transactions take place solely through state agencies, occasionally on the basis of barter. This meant that functionaries decided which of their country's products should be sold abroad, at what price or in exchange for what. When functionaries attempt to replace the workings of the market the results are always inefficient and frequently disastrous. Ethiopian officials bought consignments of Scotch whisky at a time when parts of the country were stricken with dire famine.

When individuals freely exchange goods or services both sides benefit because they have gained from the particular skills, equipment or resources of the other party. The goods or services I make and sell represent a certain amount of my time and energy. The items I buy in exchange have a higher value to me in terms of time and energy or I would not make the exchange. Sometimes I might try to make the product myself but mostly I can't. To learn to do so would be time-consuming so I do not attempt to learn the skills. A blacksmith can make horseshoes, not bread; a baker can make bread, not horseshoes.

Suppose now that the personal and natural energy required to make one horseshoe is exactly the same as for one loaf of bread, the blacksmith and baker can exchange one horseshoe for one loaf of bread and both are better off. Both have special skills and special equipment. If the blacksmith had made the loaf of bread and the baker the horseshoe, each would have taken much longer even assuming that the finished result was as good. The same is true when countries trade with each other, each using their competitive advantage which may be raw materials, cheaper labour or better know-how. Trade at all levels increases utility for all concerned.

The simple example of the blacksmith and the baker demonstrates the classic argument for free trade. It also explains why people choose different occupations. The blacksmith may have inherited his forge and he may have been taught his trade by his father, but if he believed he could earn more by being a baker he would sell his forge and buy a bakery. In doing so, he would have to learn new skills and this would represent a cost to him in terms of time and energy, but he would expect this initial investment to be compensated later by his bakery earning him more than his forge.

If the blacksmith and baker were both students with no businesses to inherit and no training for either trade, they would choose the trade that seemed most suited to their inclinations and abilities. The blacksmith might be particularly strong. The baker might be partial to bread. If neither had any such predispositions they would both choose the trade in which they expected to obtain the best return in money — which is to say claims on other people's time and energy or on finished goods and services — in return for their own time and energy. This would be strongly influenced by the number of other bakers and blacksmiths in the community.

Let us suppose that both students see that bakers are making a lot of money and that blacksmiths are doing badly, as economic men both will become bakers. So too will many others who have made the same observation and come to the same decision. For a time therefore a large number of new bakers will set up in business and no new blacksmiths. In order to compete, the larger number of bakers will have to share a total bread market — let us assume it to be of constant size. They compete on price because they know that consumers choose a given commodity at the lowest price available. All earn less money and some go out of business. At this point college students notice that bakers are doing less well than blacksmiths and choose to become blacksmiths. Before long the market determines a new balance between blacksmiths and bakers.

The fact of trading in the market provides signals to all concerned both as to the goods which are required by consumers now and as to the occupations which people should undertake to supply those goods and services in future. Trade is the essential way of showing everyone what to do if they are to maximise their net receipts of energy or utility in a given time. The period of time may be taken as that of a working life, but these days shorter horizons of three to five years may be the yardstick.

Money is the standard form of wage though by no means the only one. Remuneration may take the form of a company car, health insurance or other perks. However, money is the basis of virtually all pay and we shall consider it in the next chapter.

Individuals think in terms of their pay. Companies think in terms of profit. The two concepts have much in common. Economic man chooses his occupation and, if he is an employee, receives a certain amount of money in return for an agreed number of hours. If he is self-employed, say a shop-keeper, the amount of money he takes is not an agreed amount in return for a fixed number of hours. However, with experience, the self-employed person comes to predict with reasonable assurance how many hours he has to work to earn a given amount of money.

The individual uses part of his wages to pay for his housing, heating, food, clothing and other necessities. What remains is, effectively, his 'profit'. Similarly, a company receives money for the goods or

148

services it sells, pays its wages, materials, rent, heating and so on. What remains is profit. The individual uses his profit for the non-essentials that give him pleasure. The company uses its profits either as dividends to shareholders or on expanding the business.

The economic activities of individuals and of groups of individuals as companies are driven by my core theory:

-       economic man at all times strives to maximise the money he receives in return for a given amount of his time and energy.

Thus time and energy determine:
-       an individual's choice of job; and
-       companies' choice of activity.

The profit motive, decried by some, is the common factor in determining an infinite number of individual choices and decisions and is a continuation of economic man's long inherited instinct for survival. Trade and the working of markets enable all to be better off. They enable individuals to choose careers that meet their aspirations both as economic men and, to the extent that they wish it, as spiritual men too. The absence of trade for subsistence nations prevents them from developing specialities for which their people are best suited. State trading by socialist and other forms of command economies has the effect of reducing or eliminating the benefit which accrues to individuals when they freely choose their occupations and the way in which they exchange goods and services. In command economies personal and corporate decisions as to the allocation of time and energy are always distorted by governmental intervention.

The universal collapse of socialism in eastern Europe at the end of the 1980s demonstrated the bankruptcy of economies run by dogma-based party functionaries. They had succeeded in stifling the natural instincts of economic man.

18   GOLD, MONEY, PRICES AND BANKING

Since early days money took the form of coins. Wealthy men had treasuries in which their money was stored. The development of modern banking systems began when banks and governments realised that for individuals to carry large quantities of coins was inconvenient. Instead, paper notes were issued which represented a given sum of money in the form of gold, silver or copper coins held on that person's behalf in a bank's vault. British bank notes issued by the Bank of England still carry an archaic and long-since mendacious promise, signed by the chief cashier, namely "I promise to pay the bearer on demand the sum of £10". The absurdity of the promise lies in the fact that the chief cashier does not say in what form he will pay £10.

In days when the paper money in circulation was related to the quantity of gold sovereigns held in the banks' vaults, the promise had validity. Today, if you asked the Bank of England for £10 in gold they would be unable to provide it because there are no minted gold coins of that value. Further, when gold or silver coins are struck for great occasions, they are not legal tender as a medium of exchange.

Bank-notes and the vast bulk of coins used around the world have no value in themselves. Why should governments put valuable metal into coinage when paper or cheap metal will do just as well? The bank-notes, quite literally, are not worth the paper they are printed on. Their only value is to be a claim on goods and services, namely the time and energy, of other people and suppliers.

For years economic textbooks have described money as a unit of account, a medium of exchange and a store of value. It has been said that coins were made round so they can circulate and flat so that you can pile them up! The textbook definition of money is sometimes extended to include money as a claim on resources. I suggest a new definition.

Money is a claim on capitalised or current natural energy and on other people's time and energy.

As we saw in the preceding chapter, economic man chooses the activity and occupation which pay him best by giving him the largest energy surplus for a given input of his time. A wage is a payment for personal energy expended. The wage may be given in the form of banknotes. This archaic system is now suited only to people without bank accounts or to people who operate in "alternative" economies and want to evade tax. Within the legitimate economy financial transactions can be settled by cheques, but increasing numbers of business transactions are made directly between bank accounts as figures on a computer.

The advent of direct financial transactions at corporate and retail levels coupled with plastic card payments at shop counters spell the inevitable decline of cheques and, within a decade or so, their elimination completely. A cheque has to be physically handed into a bank. With the heavily reduced number of bank branches it may have to be sent by post — another industry in permanent decline — to a payee who in turn must pay it in at a bank. The banking system still requires a minimum of three working days before the cheque is cleared in the recipient's account.

New forms of electronic money are now well established. Credit and debit cards are widely used at check-out points in supermarkets and small retailers alike. As a new development, cards no longer need to be inserted into a PIN reader. Transactions up to £15 can be scanned by passing the card over the reader like the Oyster cards on the London underground system.

Money can now be sent from one mobile to another. This system has caught on fast in Africa where there are few home computers and even fewer bank branches. In essence, traditional money in the form of notes and coins is set to decline.

My definition of money does not contradict the traditional descriptions but extends and improves them considerably. Consider the three traditional definitions of money, given above.

Money, a unit of account
When people travel abroad, they expect to find different money and different coins and banknotes. Quickly the traveller learns to think in the new unit of account. Whether the unit is a £ sterling, a euro, a US dollar or Swiss franc, what matters is what you can buy locally with the claims on time and energy that you carry in your wallet.

Money, a medium of exchange
Apart from notes and coin, you can write cheques or make payments by numerous plastic cards. You can instruct your bank over the telephone or by Internet connection to make payments. All these newer forms of payment are aimed to increase the convenience of monetary exchanges.

Money, a store of value

Although money, whether in physical form or as numbers on a bank statement, has no intrinsic value, it remains a claim on other people's time and energy in whatever form providing that all users have confidence in its retaining its value. Since earliest days men have used gold and silver as money. The initial reason must have been that these two metals were aesthetically beautiful. Gold in particular did not tarnish. Both were soft and could be readily made into jewellery.

The supply of gold and silver has always been limited and extracting them from the ground remains costly in terms of time and energy. The gold-rushes of history have seen men using considerable time and personal energy digging mines with pick-axes and panning for gold in running water. Modern gold mines use heavy and sophisticated mining equipment and the world's most accessible deposits of gold have been found.

Because supplies of gold and silver were limited they readily became a store of value. Whether they were kept as coins or made into artefacts, the shortage of new supplies of gold and silver meant that they maintained their value. This being so they could readily be exchanged for other items. Soon they became a widely accepted as a new commodity, money. Rulers saw the advantage of coins and began to mint them officially. People found that money was a more convenient medium of exchange than barter, so coins became acceptable as a means of paying for goods or services.

From early days low value coins were made of a lower value metal, typically copper. When minted, a coin was given a denomination as some fraction of a silver or gold coin and came to have a higher usefulness than its value as metal alone. Thus, the confidence that people had in copper coins as a medium of exchange derived from their confidence in gold and silver coins. Gold and silver were prized in their own right so coins of gold and silver were accepted as a store of value. When melted down, they maintained their value providing their purity was assured.

Gold retains a function as money to this day because some international debts between nations are still settled in gold. Gold ingots are held in the Bank of England, Fort Knox, the Federal Reserve Bank's underground vault in Manhattan and in other safe places. Periodically, ingots are wheeled around the vaults and placed on different stacks to reflect transactions between national central banks.

Gold and paper money
In theory any commodity can be used as money: shells for example. Money, when suitably printed, is difficult to counterfeit but as a rule governments control the printing presses so if they choose to print an abundance of money its usefulness as a store of value falls. This is known as inflation. In Germany during the 1920s, in various Latin American countries at different times, in Serbia in 1994 and in Zimbabwe during the 2000s inflation was experienced at 1000% or more per year.

Gold, as the most valuable metal known to early man, was functional for making jewellery as well as coins. More recently, because it does not tarnish it has been used in the contacts of electronic microcircuits. Gold will continue to be mined and refined so long as governments and private citizens trust it as a store of value.

As well as gold, certain currencies are also used as stores of value, for example the US$, the Swiss Franc, the Euro and the Japanese Yen. Banks, investing institutions and private speculators swap holdings of these currencies when they expect their value to change against each other, and they buy gold particularly at times of international crisis when they cannot be sure that any of the currencies will hold their value against gold.

All currencies have a value in terms of gold even though in most countries gold is not legal tender. The security of gold is that it has to be mined. Despite modern mining technology, this is a laborious business. Many tonnes of ore have to be mined and refined to produce an ounce of gold. Unless new deposits are discovered unexpectedly, the world's supply of gold can be increased only slowly but predictably.

For many years the US$ was pegged to gold at the rate of US$35 per ounce of gold. For a number of reasons, in 1971 this artificial relationship was abandoned and the US$ was allowed to move freely to find the market price at which investors chose to exchange gold for the US$. It became unfashionable to suggest a return to the gold standard in which the amount of money in circulation was related to the amount of gold held by a country's central bank.

There were two reasons. First, politicians, economists and others felt that it was unnecessary to be constrained by the availability of gold. Control of the money supply was seen as an important way of influencing the economy. While the quantity of gold in central banks' vaults was determined largely by international transactions settled in gold, the quantity of money in the economy was determined by the government's printing press, its taxes and its borrowing. Since politicians see their reason for existing as the desire to influence other people's lives they were unwilling to see the role of gold increased and their powers correspondingly diminished.

The second disadvantage of gold was that two of the world's main suppliers were South Africa and Russia. For many years both were seen as reprehensible regimes. However, the dramatic years of 1989 onwards saw the crumbling of apartheid and the establishment of democracy in Russia.

Because the quantity of the world's gold stock cannot be manipulated, gold has historically been considered the money of last resort. Yet this is illogical. As noted earlier, all forms of money have one purpose only: to be a claim on time and energy in some form. Time is intangible so it seems clear that *natural energy should be the money of last resort.*

Currencies of last resort

Let us consider the relative importance and value of three commodities:

1) gold;
2) currency printed on paper and computer screens; and
3) energy.

Now, let us imagine three cases. In each case, a magician makes one of the three commodities disappear instantly from the world.

On the first day the magician waves his wand and gold disappears. People awake to find that every gold ring has gone from their fingers, Fort Knox is empty and the gold plating on electronic circuits and taps in rich bathrooms has disappeared.

What happens? Very little. There would be a relative injustice between nations and individuals who had stored their claims on energy in the form of gold. Some men and many women would feel bereft of their jewellery. The performance of some electronic equipment would become less reliable and dentists would use other materials to crown teeth. However, the same amount of energy would be available in the world and trading using paper money and computer screens would continue. After a period of adjustment as individuals and nations found that some of their assets had disappeared, the world would continue much as before.

On a second day, the magician waves his wand. He restores gold but all other forms of money disappear overnight. Paper notes and coins would disappear and computer screens of bank accounts would be blank. The consequences would chaotic and far far more so than the loss of gold. Bank statements would become blank statements. People would immediately start to trade by barter. Fraud would be rife and there could be civil unrest until a new currency was printed. However, power stations would still function, the lights would remain on, cars would drive and planes would fly. Life would revert to normal after a very painful period of adjustment.

The magician waves his wand a third time. All forms of money are restored but in a trice all forms of natural energy disappear except the sun. The lights go out. All transport grinds to a halt. All communication apart from the human voice stops. All production stops. Homes go cold and in many parts of the world people freeze to death within days. There is no transport other than on animals. Those with sailing yachts would make a dash for warmer climes. In short, civilisation as we know it would shudder and in parts of the world would cease altogether. Populations would try to migrate to hotter regions to eke out a lifestyle reminiscent of the Middle Ages but with no power driven transport few would make it. There would be intense hardship and perpetual conflict resulting from the breakdown of law and institutions.

From the three examples it follows that *energy should be the currency of final resort.*

At this point readers will say: "but there is no magician about to abolish natural energy." No indeed, but in his place economic man is exhausting nature's capital energy at a spendthrift rate and is not yet making sufficient efforts to replace it with natural current energy. All of us as economic people are collectively waving the magician's wand and we prefer not to notice what we are doing.

A currency denominated in Roines
Let us now take further the concept that in future all paper currencies should be denominated in units of energy such as kilowatt-hours. For fun I propose to call the new currency the **Roine**. Firstly, our energy bills would be inflation proofed. If we used 100 units of electricity in a month, we would pay 100 Roines. If we earned 100 Roines we would always be able to buy 100 units of electricity or a constant number of litres of petrol or of crude oil. Each unit of capitalised or current natural energy bought by a Roine would have

the same energy equivalent.

Roines would have the attraction that, like gold, the amount available in the world would depend on liftings of oil and gas. Governments would find it difficult to print Roines delinquently because they would have to be convertible at any time into energy.

The total stock of Roines would depend on the known available and exploitable stock of oil, gas and coal. Instead of printing money at whim, governments would be forced to issue Roines based on the total exploitable stock of natural capital energy in their jurisdictions. The amount would vary depending on the rate of depleting existing reserves. Given that natural reserves are being depleted faster than new reserves are being discovered, the total stock of Roines would fall and other items from food through to finished products would become more expensive when valued in Roines. Consumers would be less well off in real terms because, having paid their heating bills in Roines, their remaining Roines would buy less of the other necessities of life whose price in Roines would have gone up.

The trend has begun already. As major oil and gas fields in the North Atlantic and elsewhere run down, world fuel prices measured in US$ become dearer. UK households already are having to spend more of their income on their heating bills, and this trend will continue. Fuel poverty is a flavour of the month among British politicians who blame it on the energy companies and fail to understand the longer term trend.

Many people are convinced that green energy, notably wind,water power and combustible biomass, will never be able to make up for falling reserves of fossil fuel and that atomic power is and must be the solution for keeping the lights on. As noted, the risks of atomic power following Chernobyl and Fukushima have not been fully evaluated, nor the cost and technical procedures for safely storing the spent but highly radioactive used fuel.

What would happen when a major new deposit of oil or gas is discovered? The government of the jurisdiction concerned would take account of the total of the new field in terms of its volume and the potential annual rate of extraction. Suppose that the new deposit is put at one billion litres of crude oil and that the value of the Roine has been set at one litre of crude oil. Let us also suppose that one tenth of the new deposit will be extracted for 10 years. The central bank would then be authorised to increase the stock of Roines in circulation by one tenth of a billion (100 million) in each of the next 10 years. The additional Roines in circulation would enable businesses to use more energy and individuals to be better off. Cheaper energy bills stimulate economic growth just as, conversely, more expensive energy reduces growth and reduces utility overall.

The use of Roines in making the economy work better
The advantages of having Roines as an energy based currency would be significant. Firstly it would make "quantitative easing" — governments' euphemism for printing money — a thing of the past. Robert Mugabe took it to extremes in Zimbabwe such that golf-players preferred to pay for their drinks before the round knowing that the price would have gone up by the time they finished the 18th hole. In essence, it would remove governments' powers to cheat through currency manipulation.

The second important advantage is that the prices of goods and services, all of which have some natural energy content, would reflect the amount of natural energy to provide them.

Consider a car. Iron ore is mined and refined, consuming natural energy. The metal is converted into steel, rolled, pressed, cast, machined, assembled and painted. Every stage of transformation entails the use of natural energy. Other components of rubber, plastic, glass and fabric are added all of which represent inputs of natural energy. At each stage of transformation there have been some inputs of human energy too, though these are tiny compared with consumption of natural energy. At the end of the transformation process is a new car. It represents a massive investment of natural energy and a very modest investment of human energy. If its price was set in Roines it would more accurately reflect the energy cost of producing it.

The cost of petrol to drive the new car would reflect its consumption of natural current energy. As the price of oil and natural gas increases there will be continuing pressure on car-makers to manufacture more fuel-efficient vehicles. The trend is already happening.

The effect of pricing in Roines would be to make every good largely reflect its cost in the world's most precious commodity — energy.

The price of services would also be denominated in Roines. However, the underlying valuation of a fee for a service, say that of a lawyer, would be the time taken by the lawyer to qualify — that is his investment of personal time — and the amount of current time to do the work concerned.

Of course the price in Roines at which every good and service was traded would also reflect supply and demand in the market. Other factors would also come into play as they always do, for example the degree of innovation in the good or service, the quality of design and the effectiveness of the marketing. Thus markets would function as they do today but the prices in Roines attached to goods and services would bear a closer relationship to the time and energy needed to bring them to the market.

At present the world's monetary system is based on gold, which from the point of view of mankind's survival is a meaningless metal, and on various paper moneys that are subject to government manipulation and have no intrinsic value. Under a Roine pricing system the relative prices of goods and services in relation to Roines and to one another would fluctuate as now. For example, electronic goods over the past decade have fallen dramatically in nominal price and in real terms. An electronic calculator or watch that a few years ago would cost £50 can be bought for £5 today and it will have many more functions. Meanwhile inflation has meant that the purchasing ability of £1 pays for a smaller basket of other food and other goods over the period and for a smaller number of units of energy denominated in kilowatts hours, cubic metres of gas and litres of fuel at the filling station.

Governments have varying degrees of conscience about destroying the integrity of money as a store of value. Since the Second World War western governments have looked on inflation, unless it was contained to a modest two per cent a year, as an evil to be to be controlled by various means, notably control of the money supply and fiscal policy. Delinquent governments, however, have seen it as a way of reneging on their debts to investors in government securities.

What is certain is that democracy is threatened when money's role as a store of value is manipulated. People who have savings in a devaluing currency are understandably resentful. Because governments, through their printing presses, are the thieves, the individual is helpless. At present there are no laws that allow a government or central bank to be sued for perpetrating inflation. The only recourse that citizens have against delinquent governments is to remove them by the ballot box. Frequently the most delinquent governments in terms of inflation are also those who do not trouble themselves with elections. The corrupt dictatorships of South America and Africa, who at times have also been freest with the money printing presses, find elections an embarrassment. Like Robert Mugabe in Zimbabwe and Laurent Gbagbo in Ivory Coast, they permit elections, rig them and then ignore the result whatever the number of votes cast against them.

The Roine could become a world currency incapable of manipulation by any government. One Roine anywhere in the world would be exchangeable for a universal unit of energy, say one KW hour. Any country possessing natural energy would be wealthy, but that is already the case. Russia and South Africa would find that demand for gold would fluctuate as its value in Roines would be determined by demand from makers of jewellery, capped teeth and electronics equipment.

How would a Stradivarius violin or a Picasso painting be valued in terms of Roines? Such items of course have negligible energy content which would only be realised as heat if they were burned! As today, their value in Roines would be high for the same economic reasons that give them high prices today in ordinary money terms. Demand for them would remain high partly because of the pleasure they give their owners and partly as a store of value in which supply cannot be increased because their makers are dead.

The introduction of the Roine should be welcome in democracies. Private citizens would enjoy a stable currency system that could not be distorted by delinquent governments. Governments of the few remaining command economies such as North Korea would not welcome the Roine. They believe that they have the right to set prices at what they consider their citizens should pay rather than what they would freely choose if the market was permitted to work. By manipulating prices they not only distort the signals which enable individuals to make choices according to the resources available, they also arbitrarily distort individuals' claim on energy.

Governments in the former socialist states claimed that their control over prices prevented inflation. It did so but at a cost that was vast and by no means proportionate to the reward. It consisted of shops without goods to sell, long queues for the basic necessities of life, black markets for essentials, savage penalties for those who bought and sold in the black markets, ubiquitous secret police, networks of informers, labour camps, so-called psychiatric hospitals and, of course, lack of freedom to leave the country.

Even the governments of the mature democracies periodically meddle with prices. The most common way was to pass laws banning price increases or to create a variety of regulatory bodies whose functionaries were charged with holding prices down. The Roine would make such meddling impossible as the money supply would be taken out of the hands of politicians and the central bankers. The concept of Roines should be attractive to all except the politicians and the central bankers themselves.

Two possible objections to the Roine can be dealt with. The first is that the underlying stock of energy on which the Roine would represent a claim, will vary in volume as it is discovered and consumed. It might seem that gold ingots are a better store of value and claim on resources because their supply is also stable and beyond the reach of government manipulation. To set against this, politicians' and people's attention would constantly be focused on the availability of energy as expressed in Roines. As the supply of energy fell, the increasing value of the Roine in buying a given item, say a loaf of bread, would encourage people to save Roines and to economise on energy. This would be beneficial. It would encourage the installation of systems for harnessing renewable energy. Thus, each farm of wind-powered generators would represent a predictable flow of Roines for many years.

Certain technical points will need to be addressed. There will be differences in the Roine value of a barrel of oil when it is under the sea and that same barrel of oil when it is on shore and before it has been separated into its various components. I suggest that the Roine should be set at the value of oil or gas when landed. However raw natural energy is valued, it must be done transparently so that the computation of the available stock of Roines cannot be manipulated by politicians, central bankers and other functionaries.

Fracking

The availability of new sources of natural gas by the process known as "fracking" is highly topical. Environmentalists are fearful of it because the side-effects in terms of ground water pollution and potential earth tremors. If fracking goes ahead it will affect the quantity of Roines in circulation in the same way as the discovery of any new sources of oil and gas.

19   PAY, PENSIONS AND NON-EMPLOYMENT

The rate for the job
When people apply for a job they consider two aspects. The first is whether the job will satisfy their aspirations in terms of using their skills, training and experience. The second is how much they will be paid in wages and other benefits. The first of these considerations may have input from spiritual man. The second is the realm of economic man.

The importance of job satisfaction is well known to any employer. People work better and stay longer if they have job satisfaction. Some people leave a job through boredom, others because they do not get on with their supervisors or colleagues. In both cases they have lost job satisfaction. There is a trade-off between job satisfaction and the financial rewards. Some people hate their work but stay with it just for the money. Others reach retirement age and could retire comfortably yet continue to work because they enjoy it. The variety of attitudes towards work and retirement demonstrates that a job must satisfy spiritual man as well as economic man.

Different jobs have different levels of spiritual satisfaction for different people. Satisfaction is related in part to the closeness of fit between the person, his skills and his aspirations. Working on a factory production line may provide considerable job satisfaction to one person but be anathema to another. People move between jobs whenever they can improve the level of job satisfaction, the financial reward or both.

In some cases, a job represents no spiritual satisfaction whatever to a given person. In this case, by definition, he regards it purely from the point of view of economic man. He must work or he will starve. He therefore chooses the job that provides the highest net margin of energy in return for a given amount of his time. However, if spiritual man is involved in the choice of job, a trade-off may have to be made. The vocations frequently are less well paid than the qualifications of those in them would warrant. The clergy, for example, normally have at least one university degree but are paid at lowly levels.

There is reason to think that lowly paid manual jobs provide little job satisfaction. Economic man is concerned only with time and energy. In choosing between two identical manual jobs he takes the one which requires the least of his physical energy in relation to the rate per hour that he is paid. An exception can occur when one job offers more hours to be worked though at a lower rate. In this case, economic man may prefer the one with the highest total earnings rather than the highest hourly rate.

Manual workers are paid precisely for the hours they work. Indeed, their lack of commitment to the work is demonstrated by the concept of overtime that is paid at a higher hourly rate, typically at time and a half. By contrast professional jobs are always advertised on the basis of an annual salary. The hours worked are not mentioned in advertisements because it is assumed that the employee will work as hard as necessary to do the job. The company's office hours and holidays are likely to be stated in the contract of employment but the concept of being paid overtime is more likely to be replaced by performance-related bonuses. Working unpaid extra hours is accepted as normal in service industries such as advertising agencies which have deadlines to meet often for demanding clients. In the USA, banks' employees are expected to put in extra hours. Annual holidays of about two weeks are far shorter than in Europe where four weeks are standard and may be increased to five or six weeks after years of service. In Japan, long hours for junior and middle management are expected as a sign of commitment to the company.

Pensions

Pensions are deferred pay. Historically in the UK men were expected to work to 65 and women to 60. This was always an absurdity because women live longer than men. Today, in some professions a retirement age can be 60 or below but governments are increasing the age for state pensions and bringing the retirement age for women into alignment with men. In the industrialised world we see the paradox of people living longer and being healthier at 65 than a generation ago yet in some cases retiring at 60. For years civil servants in particular were paid generous pensions starting at 60 but this is being changed to bring them into line with the rest of the workforce.

It is clear that some people choose to retire early. When voluntary redundancy is offered, not uncommonly the numbers of redundancies requested is oversubscribed. This is not necessarily because those who depart expect to be able to get another job easily. It occurs at a time when unemployment is at 10% of the labour force in many industrialised countries. Instead it indicates that those seeking early retirement in their 50s have already reached a standard of living that they can maintain even on a significantly reduced income. In practical terms, they have paid off the mortgage and their children are no longer dependent.

A second aspect, unique to the era we live in, is that the speed of technological change and the stress that this causes have meant that it is common for people to pass their peak of usefulness to the organisation earlier than before. Demotion within any organisation has always been considered unacceptable, and it is not certain that those who have technologically passed their prime at a high grade would be employable even at a lower one. A bank branch manager aged 55 may be unable to handle the computer packages that present no problem to his junior staff straight from school or university. Moving older people to lower posts does not seem to be a solution. In practice, many early retirees go into freelance consultancy. This is a good solution that rewards them according to the hours they do. From their clients' perspective they are a resource that can be used as and when needed without adding to the payroll burden.

The pensions that organisations offer are supposed to bear some relationship to the employee's earnings and what he has paid into the scheme. In practice, many pension schemes are archaic and unjust in this respect. In a correctly working scheme, individuals pay into a pension scheme some part of their wages. These payments usually have an employer's contribution added. The funds paid in thus should be placed in a personal account for the employee. The entire pension fund should be invested carefully and, ideally, to bear interest that will keep up with inflation. On retirement, the employee may convert his personal pension pot into an annuity which is paid to him for the rest of his life. There is an element of luck here, for his life expectancy is unknown, but actuaries ensure that the fund which provides the annuity can balance long lives against short.

Pension schemes, whether private or run by the state, generally do not conform to the most fundamental concept that a pension is personal to the employee and is the equivalent of his savings. One commonly used system was that the employee's pension was based on the number of years in the scheme and his final salary. This meant that those who rose fastest and ended up best paid got more from the scheme than their payments warranted, and the plodders got less. There is no logic or justice in this form of redistribution of wealth and in recent years a large number of schemes based on final salary have been phased out. Inevitably, functionaries and MPs have no qualms about clinging on to such grossly inequitable schemes that they have awarded themselves.

A further objectionable feature of these systems is that some do not allow a transfer value when the employee changes jobs, or if they do, the transfer value may be lower than the payments made. This effectively constitutes a fine on those who leave. For many years the British civil service allowed no transfer value whatever on the grounds that they had paid no pension contributions. Those who left might be permitted to leave behind them a "frozen" pension based on their departing salary. This in turn would be whittled away by inflation and the absence of promotion. By contrast, those who stayed the course as functionaries were awarded index-linked pensions paid by successive governments, some of which have presided over massive inflation. In short, the concept of a pension as compulsorily deferred pay has been violated over the years, not least in the UK by governments guided by expediency rather than justice. However, the trend is for pension pots to become "portable" so that is becomes easier to move between jobs. A flexible labour market is an important aspect of a healthy economy.

In third-world countries state or private pension systems are less common or non-existent. For this reason in Africa large families are seen as a pension. Western economic man stores energy in the form of money against the day when he no longer will work. African villagers store energy in the form of children who will look after them when they can no longer work.

Non-employment
A retired person is normally non-employed, though some retired people find paid work and many do voluntary work. A person who is unemployed by definition is of working age. The distinction between being unemployed and retired for people in their 50s and early 60s is becoming increasingly blurred. Some non-employed people genuinely seek work while others are content to live on unemployment benefit, the equivalent of an early state pension. Some early retired people also genuinely seek work but others are content to live on their savings. The industrialised world therefore witnesses a new phenomenon: an increasing group of able-bodied people in their 50s and 60s who are at leisure, consuming and not producing but who are living longer than ever before. Why is this?

The reason lies in economic man's success in finding and harnessing natural energy. From the earliest days of the steam age, machines have replaced people to do jobs that required manual effort, and the same continues today as robots in factories replace humans' physical energy and computers replace humans' brain power. The availability of abundant, cheap natural energy for 50 years occurred at the same time as the most extraordinary invention in the history of mankind: the transistor which is the basis of the digital computing revolution and all that goes with it.

Machines and robots have not merely replaced human effort; they have enabled man to do things far better, faster and more accurately than would be possible with bare hands guided by human brains. Machines build machines. Robots build more robots. Computers design new generations of computers. Humans design the software but are helped to do so by the vast bases of existing software. Thus today's software creates yet more sophisticated software for the next generation of computers, the processor chips and the memories that power them.

And what happens when there is a power cut? Every computer screen goes blank. The vast quantities of information stored in computers are irretrievable without electricity. Robots and other machines stop working, all office equipment and every home appliance goes dead. Most trains stop. Cars run until the tank is empty and then stop because the pumps at filling stations do not work. In minutes or hours, without energy, our industrial society grinds to a halt.

Of course, all is not quite as perilous as I have described. In reality, back-up generators switch into action and power is restored. But if the power supply dwindles over time instead of being cut at a stroke, there will soon be not enough natural energy to move the trains and power the robots. Computers themselves take little energy to run, so they will still be able to function even if electrical power is in short supply, just as a brain can function even if the body is short of food.

However, without robots manual work will increase. Household appliances will become more costly to buy and run so people will begin to wash clothes and dishes by hand again. The pool of unemployed or early retired will be absorbed by the new demands for services requiring human energy.

The question of non-employment is seen to be directly linked to the availability of natural energy. While the latter remains plentiful, non-employment will remain widespread. Politicians and others who seek to find ways to regain full employment as exemplified by a conventional 40-hour week, will not be able to do so. At best they will find ways to spread non-employment more widely. Job-sharing, early retirement and part-time working will continue to be the natural consequence of abundant natural energy coupled with man's power to think and create. We are already in the era of significant non-employment including both retirement and unemployment, but it will last only as long as the golden age of cheap natural energy. Cheap oil and gas-based energy is dwindling but this will create opportunities for low level services such as gardening and sweeping streets.

20   POWER OVER THINGS AND PEOPLE

Since earliest times man needed territory to survive. Territory gave him hunting rights and land for cultivation. When his primary needs of food, clothing and shelter had been satisfied he came to desire artefacts. Initially each primitive man made his own artefacts: his spear, pots, skin clothes and axe. When more skills were needed, people specialised in particular crafts and exchanged what they made, so the concept of trading began. The invention of sailing boats greatly extended the region over which trade could take place. Individuals were all better off by trading those goods that they had in plentiful supply in exchange for those from another community or country that were obtainable only or much more cheaply there.

Artefacts give economic man pleasure. The earliest artefacts — flint knives to cut with and stone axes to hunt with — helped make his life easier. In a similar way modern economic man looks on possessions as a source of happiness and as a symbol of success. Sometimes they are a store of value and a form of insurance against the future — paintings by famous artists, for example. In general, economic man is never satisfied with his possessions. If he has ten shirts, he may still buy an eleventh which takes his fancy. His car may be only a few years old but he trades it in for the latest model.

As people grow older, economic man sometimes gives ground to spiritual man, and sexual man also diminishes in importance. People's bodies become less energetic. The attraction of working hard to add to possessions appeals less to economic man when he sets a higher value on free time and conserving personal energy. Spiritual man is unaffected by a decline in the body's physical energy.

Indeed, lack of physical energy, even infirmity, can heighten the spiritual dimension in people as they age.

There is no consistent pattern but some people mellow in old age. If they have achieved the goods and lifestyle they want their economic dimension declines. When a person's spiritual dimension exceeds his economic dimension, his desire for possessions decreases. Old people often refuse to acquire new possessions they could easily afford. They feel comfortable with what they already have and understand. Why spend precious time learning how to use a new cooker when the old one still cooks adequately?

In general, the dominance of spiritual man over economic man does not occur until people are 60 or more and in some people this dominance never happens. From the 60s and 70s onwards death becomes a reality which previously could be ignored in the pressure of everyday living. It is no coincidence that most people in industrialised countries have traditionally retired between 60 and 65. At this age their minds are still sharp but their economic dimension has diminished. They no longer seek to acquire things for the sake of doing so. Those who stay in work beyond 65 are generally people whose work is with the mind – judges, conductors and academics for example.

Economic man is acquisitive and likes to acquire possessions and claims on the services of people. In earliest days primitive man did his own work. Later he domesticated beasts of burden as a substitute for his own physical energy. From early times the concept of slavery was invented by economic man. Slaves were an alternative source of energy with major advantages over animals because of their intelligence. Slaves worked the cotton fields and sugar plantations of the USA and elsewhere until the abolition of slavery.

The concept of slavery as something reasonable lasted until the early 1800s in Europe. Economic man saw the benefit of slavery, providing he was the master. The abolition of slavery coincided in Europe with the start of the industrial revolution. Labour was still cheap but the invention of the steam power began to replace craftsmen by machines. Economic men, at least those who were rich, possessed large numbers of servants. They were not slaves in a legal sense but in the early years many including all women were without the vote. Further, since there was no unemployment pay and the workhouse was an unappealing prospect, servants and employees were beholden to their employers economically if not legally. Spiritual man may have wished to treat his employees well. Economic man in general did not. Women pulled coal trucks in the mines and small boys were sent up chimneys to sweep them.

In western Europe the First World War and the impact of the Russian revolution brought the first major crack in capitalists' power over people. In the 1920s women in Britain won the vote, trade unions were recognised and a Labour government came to power. In the labour market periods of high unemployment and the absence of social security meant that wealthy people still had immense power over the poor. Servants remained cheap. Employees could be sacked on the spot and good references were essential to find another job. In the country, land owners controlled access to the land's food energy. In cities, mill owners controlled access to steam energy. There was a surplus of labour so wages were low and needed only to be somewhat above subsistence level.

The Second World War and the electric motor changed all that. Compulsory conscription removed most male servants overnight. Female servants went to the factories to replace the men who had been called up. After the war electricity began to replace servants. Vacuum cleaners replaced maids with dustpans and brushes. Gas and electricity replaced coal fires for servants to light and tend. Electric irons replaced those heated on coal hobs and washing machines replaced washerwomen. By the 1970s only the seriously wealthy had permanent servants and progress towards replacing human time and energy with machines in the home continued unabated. In the 1970s dishwashers began to replace manual washing up and in the 1980s onwards microwave ovens allowed new forms of instant cooking.

Servants who had left domestic employment went to factories, shops and offices where they could be controlled by economic man as before. Economic man's desire to dominate others remained deeply entrenched. In most organisations promotion meant power over people. It also entailed spending less personal energy. Supervisors watched while operatives expended energy. Promotion also entailed more pay — more claims on the energy of others. In short, when economic man sought to replace his own energy he did so by using slaves, serfs, servants and finally employees or subordinates.

Politics as a means to power
After economic man has attained food, clothing, shelter and basic material possessions he seeks services. Power over people is fifth in the hierarchy of economic man's desires but it is increasingly important when the first four have been satisfied.

Power over people is the prime motivation in politics. At election time politicians claim fulsomely that their aim is to *serve* voters. When elected their real aim is to *dominate* voters as well as getting as much money out of the system as possible. The ceaseless flood of legislation imposed by politicians and their functionaries in democratic countries is the clear proof of their desire to control other people's lives but frequent and continuing corruption and expenses-rigging scandals in industrialised and developing economies alike prove their real, venal motives for being in politics at all.

Most politicians end their careers wealthier than they would otherwise have been, often considerably so. In corrupt nations rulers and their families become ultra-wealthy thanks to the spoils of power and corruption. In the banana republics of Latin America and Africa, politics is about the quest for wealth and the goal is a big Swiss bank account. Wealth and politics both mean the power to claim the energy of others. The quest for political power and the quest for wealth are complementary and appeal to the same sort of people. Some rich men enter politics, particularly in the USA where money and power are virtually synonymous. In 1992 Ross Perot, a tiny, unknown multimillionaire made a credible attempt to become president of the USA. Having attained material goods and services through the power of money, politicians seek a different kind of power, the power to control other people's lives.

Should politics be the field of spiritual man rather than economic man? Probably not. The intolerance and cruelty of the ayatollahs in Iran and their spiritual forebears in the Christian churches of Europe from the crusades to the late Middle Ages, suggest that spiritual men, assuming these people are or were indeed spiritual, make bad politicians. A few exceptions can be found but they are few. Mahatma Gandhi and Martin Luther King were major spiritual and political figures who chose non-violent means to advance their campaigns and for whom there was no apparent financial motivation. For every Gandhi and King there have been innumerable politicians worldwide who, before being driven from office, have transferred liberal helpings from the public purse to their Swiss bank accounts through corruption or simple theft from the public treasury.[8]

In practice it seems inevitable that politics should be the field of economic and not spiritual man. Since economic man is motivated by self-interest, the necessary framework to prevent self-interest becoming corruption is democracy and a free press.

---

[8] See Ian Senior (2006), *Corruption: the World's Big C.* Institute of Economic Affairs

21   DEMOCRACY AND SOCIALISM

Words have no absolute meaning. Their meaning is established by usage and context. Dictionaries define the meaning of words as understood by the compilers at the time, but language is a living thing and meanings change. For example, the Concise Oxford Dictionary's fourth edition, 1950, provides the following definitions of the word 'gay', in this order and slightly abbreviated:

- full of mirth
- cheeky
- (slang) immoral, living by prostitution, showy, brilliant,
- brightly coloured, finely dressed.

Today the word gay has one primary meaning as a noun or an adjective, namely a male homosexual — which does not appear in the 1950 edition of the dictionary.

This brief excursion into the meaning of words is necessary because both democracy and socialism mean different things to different people. The former state of East Germany — along with other former communist regimes of east Europe — called themselves "democratic". In the United Kingdom a centrist political party calls itself the Liberal Democrats. The USA's Democratic Party's policies would be described as right-wing in some other countries.

I suggest seven tests of what constitutes true democracy. They are:

1   universal adult suffrage
2   freedom to form political parties

3   secret ballots

4   voting without intimidation or bribery

5   fixed term elections at intervals not chosen by those in power

6   independent and free news media

7   proportional representation.

Tests 1-4

Tests 1 to 4 seem to me to be self-evident and to need no justification.

Test 5

Test 5 — elections at intervals not chosen by those in power — is clearly essential. To be able to choose the timing of elections is to manipulate the system. Politicians can and do call elections unashamedly when opinion polls give them the best chance of success. For many years the British electoral system and those derived from it failed to qualify as democratic by test 5 but the current coalition government very rightly has set five year fixed term parliaments.

Test 6

Test 6 — independent and free news media — also seems to me to be self-evident. A question here arises over the extent to which the press in western democracies is in fact part of the political system, economically biased and thus distorting rather than enhancing democracy.

Can the media influence the result of elections? This seems highly likely, at least where the result is going to be close. If businessmen find that advertising influences the sale of their products, so political advertising equally must influence the votes of the electorate. In the UK for many years and fairly recently in the USA, financial limits have been imposed on expenditure by politicians during their election campaigns.

Such limits do not cover editorial. Partisan newspapers can and do emphasise particular stories. For example a trivial gaffe or slip of the tongue by a politician can become headline news or buried in the middle pages. The private lives of politicians can be raked over in the glare of publicity as a matter of public comment even when this has nothing to do with their suitability to run the country. The promiscuous Lloyd George and John F Kennedy would not have achieved their offices if the press of the day had allowed itself to report on their private lives.

In the UK a number of prominent politicians have seen their careers ruined by investigative reporting of their infidelities. In Italy, by contrast, the sexual escapades attributed to Silvio Berlusconi appear to be ignored or admired by a large part of the population. In addition, Berlusconi is a major media magnate himself who controls three out of seven national television channels and is thus able to control or suppress negative comment about his private life.

The stories, photographs, and quotations attributed to politicians and the headlines can and do have bias according to the views of the proprietors and their editorial staff. In the UK Lord Levison's enquiry following the telephone hacking scandals shone a bright light on the closeness of prime ministers, ministers and other senior politicians to the now defunct *News of the World* and on Rupert Murdoch's media empire generally.

What needs to be done to ensure that the media contribute to, rather than detract from, the workings of democracy? One simple safeguard would be for individuals or organisations to be able to extract significant damages for *inaccuracy* as an actionable offence in its own right. It should not be necessary for the injured party to prove libel or even financial damage. Once newspapers learned that they could be fined for inaccuracy pure and simple they would have to adopt higher standards of reporting or suffer the consequences. One of Levison's major recommendations was indeed the concept of punitive damages. The path has already been prepared by damages running to many millions of pounds against Murdoch's papers for telephone hacking.

Any alternative involving government control of the media is clearly unacceptable within the context of British democracy. The role of inaccuracy and defamation on the social networks, notably Facebook and Twitter, is in process of being established by individual cases rather than legislation. By contrast, France for many years exercised political control over its broadcasting authorities. Control of broadcasting and newspapers is standard practice in dictatorships including Arab and African states.

Test 7

The final test, proportional representation, may be the most controversial of my seven tests of democracy. Proportional representation means that the composition of an elected chamber closely reflects the proportion of votes cast for the parties represented in it. The British voting system abysmally fails this test of democracy. Generally known as "first past the post", the British system means that the political party which wins the largest number of members of parliament forms the government even if its proportion is well under half the votes cast. In the UK, for decades governments have swung between Labour and Conservative with the winning party having less than 40 per cent of the votes cast. This has given rise to changes of policy that have been far too abrupt because the voting system gives rise to completely unjustified "working majorities".

Proponents of the British system claim that it provides strong government and point to the short-lived and supposedly ineffective coalitions produced by Italy's proportional electoral system. By contrast, however, a system of proportional representation is used in Germany and has produced stable — many would say excellent — government since the war. Ironically, the German system was installed by the British as one of the victorious Allies in 1945.

Opponents of the British system point out that it penalises minorities and produces majorities which bear little relationship to the numbers of votes cast — two serious defects. A further defect is that the system gives wide scope for "gerrymandering", the device by which electoral boundaries are drawn or changed to influence the result of the election. For example, in the first years of the present British coalition government the British boundaries were in the process of being redrawn so that the number of electors in each constituency was about the same. Cynically, and following party political machinations, the Liberal Democrats in the coalition government joined with Labour in having the implementation of boundary changes postponed until after the 2015 election. Both parties believed they would benefit electorally by this chicanery. By contrast, the Conservative party which repeatedly since World War II had benefitted from the first-past-the-post system now foresees the possibility that it could lose power to a new coalition of Liberal Democrats and Labour after the general election in May 2015.

The British, US and Canadian electoral systems and those derived from the British system, fail the seventh test of democracy.

Other arguments favour proportional representation. Coalitions can be beneficial in producing centrist and moderate governments. Partnerships between groups of people are found to be honourable when they are called firms or companies. Partnerships between countries are honourable when they are called economic communities, associations or alliances. It seems strange therefore that partnerships, temporary or otherwise, between political parties should be considered dishonourable by some. Such partnerships entail compromise and collaboration and reflect the reality of human relations at all levels.

The argument that non-proportional systems produce firm government is based on the flawed premise that "strong government" is intrinsically desirable. Dictatorships of the South American, African and Arab/Muslim model certainly constitute "strong government" but are repellent in many ways. The extraordinary uprisings in Tunisia, Egypt, Libya, Syria, Yemen and Bahrain in the Arab Spring of 2011 arose directly from the governance of dictators who tried hard to cling to power. Unarmed demonstrators were shot in public and others were arrested by the security services only to disappear in prison. Torture of political opponents was routine. Even doctors who tended the wounded at demonstrations were bundled away by state security and disappeared.

Politicians given large majorities of members of parliament by non-proportional voting systems ignore the number of votes cast and believe they have a mandate to impose legislation which may be unpalatable to well over half the voters. By contrast, proportional representation eliminates "strong" government and replaces it by "reflective" government that more accurately reflects the way electors voted. This is what democracy should mean.

Applying the tests
Of the seven tests, I suggest that the first four are decisive and that any electoral system which does not pass all four simultaneously cannot be described as democratic. Therefore all communist states including China, most black African and several South American states fail to qualify as democracies. Up to the Arab spring of 2011 the entire Middle East apart from Israel failed to qualify under tests 1-4. Most countries in the region are now moving towards more freedom and democracy. Syria and Iran are the main exceptions.

Tests 5-7 are important but countries such as the USA and France which fail one of the tests could perhaps be described as flawed democracies. The UK's national system fails two tests. The House of Commons is elected by first-past-the-post or simple majority. The House of Lords is unelected. Some members are still there on the basis of birthright. Most of the others are there by political patronage. None has been elected.

Curiously, the central government in Westminster imposed proportionality on the voting systems used for the Scottish parliament and the Welsh assembly. Another form of proportional voting, the Alternative Vote, was heavily defeated in a British national referendum in 2012.

In non-democratic countries inefficiency, abuse of power, corruption, injustice, police brutality and absence of human and civil rights are normal. But why are there so few democracies?

In dictatorships the rulers are always wealthy, the ruled poor. The gap between the wealthy and the poor is always much larger than in democracies. The rulers correctly believe that if democracy is permitted, their personal wealth will be reduced or seized and that, worse still, they will be held accountable for their past actions in acquiring it.

One of the outstanding results of the Falklands war in 1982 was the subsequent returning of Argentina to a faltering democratic process with free elections. This consequence must have come as a shock to General Galtieri and the junta of military rulers who during a decade of the "dirty war" were responsible for the torture and death without trial of thousands of political opponents. Removed from office, tried and found guilty, the members of the junta were treated under democracy with astonishing leniency given the nature of their crimes. Had they been treated as were thousands under their regime, they would have been tortured to death in some squalid cell. Torture and legal execution play a far more limited and, it is to be hoped, waning role in democracies.

Philosophers have played their part in obstructing democracy. The writings of Karl Marx and Lenin gave dictators in the USSR, China, Africa, North Korea and Cambodia the justification for imposing despotic rule in the name of socialism. The writings of Chairman Mao justified the Cultural Revolution which caused chaos and mass killings in China from 1966 onwards. Conversely the most unpleasant right-wing regimes of Latin and South America justified their despotic rule by the need to prevent takeovers by communists. As Orwell brilliantly depicted in *Animal Farm* there is no difference in the aims or methods used by dictatorships of the far left or the far right.

Religions have also played a role in obstructing the advent of democracy. Christianity tolerated slavery for many centuries up to the nineteenth. Islam is considered an acceptable basis for quasi dictatorship throughout most of the Middle East, notably by governments such as those of Iran and Saudi Arabia which permit stoning to death of women (though not men or male rapists) for adultery, amputation of thieves' hands and other medieval practices.

In recent years the Christian church's record on human rights has improved and it may be no coincidence that the areas of the world where electoral systems pass some of the seven tests of democracy are those with a Christian tradition.

There is a clear relationship between the way democracy and voting systems concord with my general theory of economic man. Full democracy provides the environment in which economic man flourishes best. His self-interested desire is to acquire claims on energy. Democracy allows him to do so. At the same time democracy ensures a reasonable distribution of those claims on energy. Under genuinely democratic electoral systems the parties or coalitions that win power do so by representing the views of a broad majority. They would lose power if they maintained extremes of wealth which appeal only to minorities. The result is that in democratic systems that meet all seven criteria earlier, extremes of wealth and poverty are avoided.

Theoretical socialism, in stark contrast to democracy, does not encourage economic man to acquire claims on energy and may be a concept that appeals to spiritual man for that reason. "To each according to his needs; from each according to his ability" presupposes that there is no relationship between the time and energy that individual economic men spend on a given piece of work. Because economic man is dominant over spiritual man, socialism where it has been tried has proved disastrous both for individuals and for states.

Joseph Stalin, in the name of socialism, sent millions of Russians to death in labour camps. In the 1970s Pol Pot's infamous regime in Cambodia murdered one third of the population in his killing fields. Before the revolutions of 1989 the socialist states of Eastern Europe required vast networks of secret police and informers to maintain the regimes in power. In the People's Republic of China, by far the largest remaining socialist state, human life remains cheap. The police shoot people suspected of petty crimes with a single bullet in the back of the head.

The gradual introduction of market forces in China has given rise to its phenomenal rise as the world's biggest manufacturing economy.

By contrast, in states such as North Korea and Cuba functionaries decide what shall be made, by whom, at what price and in what quantities. The result has been starvation to death of millions in North Korea and perennial rationing in Cuba.

In a collectivist society an economic man who works hard has no more claims on energy than a shirker, so incentive is lost. Instead, claims on energy are given for services to the party. Socialism suppresses economic man and, as practised, cannot satisfy spiritual man because the latter realises that without freedom of thought and deed, there can be no spiritual satisfaction. When socialist regimes fall, it is common to discover that the leaders have been economic men all along. The vast palace built by Ceausescu in Romania, and the luxurious secret dwellings of Honeker's ministers in East Germany show the workings of economic man within the trappings of socialism. Even the current leaders of the PRC admit that tackling corruption must be one of their priorities and have to turn a blind eye to the fortunes that their predecessors have accumulated in office.

Socialist regimes do not allow people to vote freely and secretly through the ballot box or to vote with their feet by leaving the country. East Germans were contained by the Berlin wall. When North Vietnam won the civil war the South Vietnamese took to ramshackle boats to escape the country. For half a century since Castro seized power, Cubans have been using little boats to flee to Florida.

By contrast citizens of democracies can travel abroad for business or pleasure without hindrance. They are free to visit socialist countries including China, Cuba and Vietnam though not North Korea. If they apply to become residents in such countries they do not have to beg political asylum. Their goods at home are not seized and their families are not arrested.

In his quest for claims on energy economic man thrives under democracy. Socialist man is a drone species. His concern is with political dogma and not with the creation of wealth; with how the cake shall be divided and not by how it shall be baked.

Democracy and dictatorship under whatever names are polar opposites. Since most men are economic most of the time the future for democracy is ultimately assured. China and Vietnam are introducing market principles to their economies with conspicuous success. Cuba is attempting to court western tourists to bring foreign currency to a bankrupt economy. Put simply, socialism doesn't work. It is contrary to the natural instinct of economic man. The writings of Karl Marx and others have had influence far more profound than could have been expected given that they are based on so fundamentally a flawed view of mankind.

To recognise the nature of economic man is to accept the need for sound democracy based on the seven principles given earlier. Without democracy economic man will exploit his fellows as ruthlessly as noblemen exploited serfs in the Middle Ages and American land-owners exploited African slaves in the eighteenth and nineteenth centuries. Since democracy constrains the activities of economic man and has only slight relevance to sexual man, it follows that the concept and implementation of democracy are the work of spiritual man. This gives hope for the future.

22   GOVERNMENT, LAWS AND TAXATION

All forms of human conduct are governed by rules. Rules are applied by children in the games they play. Team sports have rules and a referee to enforce them. Clubs, societies and groups of every sort impose rules so that members know where authority and responsibility lie.

Nation states are like any other group of people who freely associate and agree to impose rules on themselves. The rules are called laws and lay down certain activities or behaviours that are not acceptable and incur penalties for breaking them. Most laws are of the "thou shalt not" variety, but some are "thou shalt" and impose obligations on citizens to perform certain tasks such as filing a tax return or doing jury service.

In a perfect society written rules might not be needed but since the earliest days of civilisation man has found that laws must be written. Only in illiterate tribal societies are laws enshrined in custom rather than writing. However, for as long as laws have been written, questions of interpretation have arisen from which the legal profession earns its living.

The essence of law in a democracy is that it should represent the will of the majority. Socialism, other forms of dictatorship, and flawed democracies such as that of the UK all enable laws to be passed implementing the will of a minority, sometimes a small minority.

In democracies the process of legislation in theory follows a logical sequence. Periodically there is a choice of legislators by means of an election. Before the election candidates say what new laws they propose to pass or, occasionally, repeal. After the election the legislators who have the majority form a government and pass or repeal the laws described in their manifestoes. When the next election comes the voters have an opportunity to choose another set of legislators if they wish who will pass new laws and perhaps abolish some existing ones.

While this general process is accepted and understood, in democracies ordinary citizens are increasingly aware that the role of government has got out of hand. The problem is easy to diagnose. Politicians of all persuasions and the functionaries who serve them love to pass new legislation. A stream of new laws flows from the legislatures. Each one imposes compliance costs on the marketed sector of the economy and creates new jobs for functionaries to administer the laws and to regulate the productive sectors of the economy.

In some ways politicians are not to blame. A candidate whose campaign pledge to the voters was to do nothing for four or five years while drawing full salary and perks might not get elected. However, if he and his party say that their aim is to reduce the burden of government, this commands more appeal. Periodically, candidates and parties do make such promises. Both Ronald Reagan and Mrs Thatcher's administrations when seeking election proclaimed that the role of government was excessive and should be diminished. Mrs Thatcher's administration returned substantial sections of industry to private ownership.

While it is clear that governments should not be involved in manufacturing and service industries of a commercial nature, a more fundamental appraisal is required of what should be the proper functions of government. A simple test helps to clarify the correct role of government:

-       if an   activity is clearly essential and benefits all equally whether they pay for it or not, then government *may* have a role to play in its provision.

Defence is a useful example. If a nation believes that it needs an army to defend its frontiers or an air force to protect its skies, all citizens benefit by that security whether they pay for it or not. Defence is known by economists as a "public good".

Other public goods can be identified, for example the police. However, just because a role for government activity has been found, it does not follow that the entire activity concerned should then be carried out by state employees. In defence, for example, quite correctly the supply of many goods and services to the army is done by private contractors. In some cases the quantity or quality of the good provided by the state is inadequate. For example police forces are overstretched in many countries, so private security firms have come into being to increase the supply of law and order.

There remain a vast range of activities currently provided by the state for historical reasons which cannot be described as public goods. Leisure centres are a case in point. There seems no reason why government, whether national or local, should supply services which, if there was demand for them, would be provided on a commercial basis.

On the contrary, there are compelling arguments why governments should *not* provide such services. Firstly, national or local functionaries are not businessmen. They are not motivated by the need to satisfy customers; they do not share in profits and losses and they earn salaries with only tenuous links to performance. If they had the inclination to be businessmen, they would not have chosen to become functionaries. Unsurprisingly, quasi-commercial operations such as leisure centres when run by functionaries often require subsidies from public funds to balance their books. This form of wealth redistribution is acceptable only if the local administration concerned has been democratically elected and stated in its manifesto that it would provide subsidised leisure centres.

Second, when functionaries run quasi-commercial operations, they are not answerable to their customers as in a business, but to politicians. In the UK a large number of elected representatives at national level have never been in the marketed sector of the economy. While most politicians wish in theory to keep taxation down, as a group they enjoy the power and influence that spending other people's money gives them.

There are certain activities in which the intervention of government is generally disastrous. Most important among these is housing. After food and clothing, housing is the third primary need. Economic man, quite properly, is concerned with ensuring that he and his dependants have all three. In a number of democracies including the UK, the state has decided to play a major role as property developer, builder and landlord for rented accommodation. In the UK the result has been a lesson from which governments elsewhere should learn. State housing has been ugly, frequently shoddy and has taken little account of the preferences of the tenants. Vast, ugly and soulless estates have been built and some have included large tower blocks. These are widely disliked by tenants but because rents have been made artificially low by subsidies, there have generally been enough would-be tenants to fill them. However, even at low rents some properties have been impossible to fill and have fallen into disrepair. Some tower-blocks have been dynamited after 15-20 years by the authorities who built them. The wasted resources of time and energy are obvious.

State housing is easily recognisable not merely because of its pervasive ugliness but also because it is badly maintained. Tenants do not own their homes and so have no incentive to maintain them. Functionaries, being both unbusinesslike and short of funds, skimp on maintenance. Properties become slums and tenants agitate for new tenancies elsewhere.

The reason for the failure of public sector housing is absurdly simple. Economic man sees no point in spending his own time and energy maintaining the property he lives in if it belongs to someone else. He has no incentive to add a value to a property that reverts to the state when he leaves. His attitude changes when he is enabled to buy that same property. On estates where some social housing properties have been sold to the tenants and others have not, the difference can be seen at once. Exteriors of the privately owned properties are painted, the gardens maintained. New doors, new porches, extensions, replacement windows, attractive and individual colours and pretty gardens stand in stark contrast to the uniformly drab and badly maintained state-owned properties beside them.

The correct role of government is to restrict its activities to the provision of public goods, notably defence and justice and to pay for these by a system of taxation that is accepted as fair by the electorate.

And what is fair? "Fairness" is one of the most commonly used clichés in a modern politician's vocabulary. I suggest that a system is *fair* only if it has been approved by a democratic voting system. The taxation system may, if the electorate approves, include mechanisms for redistributing wealth from the rich to the poor but this needs to be included in the manifesto of the governing party *before* it has a mandate to do so. For example, political parties should always publish their standard and top rates of tax including the tax thresholds before an election. For the wining party, these levels of taxation could then legitimately be described as *fair*.

It seems clear that the economic value to society of some most gifted individuals is at least 100 times higher than the least gifted. The author of a successful play, a film star, a top athlete or a successful businessman may easily earn £1-2m a year upwards. A low level worker may earn £10,000-20,000 per year, yet there can be no abstract law or rule about what is a "fair" distribution of wealth. Some people have attempted to give guidelines, for example that the ratio of the highest paid to the lowest paid in an organisation should be no more than twenty. Whether or not this is a *fair* ratio can be tested by elections but does not guarantee that supply and demand for particular skills in the labour market will balance.

In democracies the taxation system can be expected in some rough and ready way to reflect voters' wishes. At an election each economic voter has the opportunity to choose the party whose approach to income distribution coincides with his self-interest. The rich vote for the party of least redistribution, the poor for the party of most. It can readily be seen that proportional representation will produce a taxation system that most closely reflects the preferences of voters across the spectrum. If a coalition of parties forms the government it will implement a system of taxation representing a compromise between the aspirations of their respective constituencies. The largest coalition parties will have most say so the taxation system will represent their preferences more closely than those of the minority coalition members. This is far more likely to produce a *fair* taxation system than the winner-takes-all method of the British electoral system and others based on it.

Once a true democracy based on proportional representation has established a central taxation system that reflects the preferences of the coalition partners, no further forms of redistribution by individual agencies are acceptable since they introduce new and unnecessary distortions in the national distribution of wealth. Economic man performs most effectively when his motivation is undistorted by confusing and contradictory systems of redistributing wealth. In particular, complex taxes give rise to tax avoidance and evasion. These are sometimes so little apart as to be termed *tax avoison*.

Once wealth redistribution has taken place through taxation, governments should allow people to lead their lives as they wish with the minimum of state interference.

A difficulty in relation to introducing *fair* taxation is that voting in elections once every four or five years is a blunt instrument. The influence of taxpayers upon how their taxation is spent could be greatly increased if all taxpayers were given the power to allocate some part of their taxation to public sectors of their choice, for example defence, police, education or health-care. In filing a tax return each year their financial allocation would directly influence the running of the country and have a much more tangible impact than merely a cross on a ballot paper once every four or five years.

Those who do not file tax returns because their tax is collected by pay-as-you-earn could make a simple statement to HMRC enabling taxpayers to make percentage allocations of, say one tenth of their total tax to their preferred departments. To preserve reasonable continuity of government one tenth of individuals' taxes might be a workable proportion. It would be enough to put all government departments and services on their toes knowing that their budgets could be increased or reduced every year by taxpayers' power.

I suggest that the power of individual taxpayers to allocate some of their taxes would be popular and should be included in party manifestoes. Politicians initially might dislike the concept as reducing their power to allocate taxation at will but that is a strong reason in favour of the idea.

23   CRIME AND PUNISHMENT

What is a crime and why does it need to be punished? The answers to these two apparently simple questions are not obvious.

The only thing that can definitely be said about crime is that it entails an action of some sort or, in certain cases, preparation for such an action. The action must be measured against a law or rule that makes the action illegal.

Most criminal actions are the realm of economic man and have their roots in time and energy. Spiritual man may devise the crime in his mind, just as he may create a poem. A few crimes, notably rape, are clearly the actions of sexual man but the vast majority of crimes result from economic man's attempts to obtain other people's assets without having to earn them through willing exchange.

The definition of any given crime is made by the elected and recognised law-makers in the jurisdiction concerned. The laws are made by governments which may be democratically elected or dictatorships.   How the law comes into being is immaterial in defining what constitutes a crime. Clearly laws are more likely to be respected if they have been made by democratically elected legislators and enforced by legal systems and police who all are answerable within the democratic system. Laws passed by dictators may just keep the lid on the jurisdiction concerned. When they are broken by those who have suffered under them, violence is frequent. The Arab spring of 2011 onwards is a prime example.

If broken, the law entails the punishment of the person who breaks the law if he is caught. At local level, laws, bye-laws or regulations may be passed by local government. Schools, companies and clubs of every kind have rules which apply to their members.

For a law to be respected it must entail defined punishments to be imposed on those who break it and there must be a judicial system to decide whether the accused person has indeed broken the law. Laws sometimes define a range of punishments, for example a fine of up to a given maximum or a prison sentence of up to a stated number of years. Less commonly, the range of a punishment includes a minimum as well as a maximum.

The law needs to command respect so that the punishment is seen as being proportional to the crime. The concept of "a loaf of bread, off with his head" and barbaric punishments in the Middle Ages and through to the twentieth century have eased greatly in most of the civilised world. Only in some barbaric Muslim countries such as Saudi Arabia and Iran are thieves' hands amputated and women stoned to death for adultery. In tribal parts of Pakistan "honour killings" by families take place, for example the killing of young women who try to marry without parental agreement. Tribal elders have been known to order the gang rape of an innocent girl whose *brother* has been found guilty of some crime.

The term crime has overtones implying a seriously illegal action, while other words are used for minor offences, for example misdemeanour or misdeed. The terminology is unimportant. The underlying concept is universal: the more serious the crime, the heavier the punishment.

Crimes are not to be confused with sins. The latter are the province of religion. Spiritual man may believe that it is a sin to lust after someone else's wife but this has never been a crime. The act of adultery is illegal in some Muslim countries and may be punished by flogging or worse, but in the western world, though it may be grounds for divorce, it is not a crime and does not give rise to punishment. In many African and some countries Muslim countries gay sex is illegal and may carry the death penalty. Gay sex between consenting adults in private was legalised in the UK only in 1967.

Perceptions of what constitutes a crime change over time. In England up to the nineteenth century, people were hanged, flogged and imprisoned for crimes that today would be regarded as petty. Today, capital punishment has been abolished in most advanced countries. Surprisingly, it remains part of the criminal code in some states of the USA. In some countries, particularly those with Islamic law or Islamic influence, the death penalty is widespread. In Malaysia, it is mandatory for trafficking in hard drugs.

In China, a non-Islamic country, executions are defined as state secrets. There are believed to be at least 3,000 executions a year which include those executed for economic crimes. Since China's legal system is highly defective by western standards it seems likely that a significant number of innocent people have been executed. Traditionally execution was by a single bullet to the back of the head but in recent years special travelling death vans have been designed and sold to local authorities. Death is by lethal injection inside the vans and the fresh body parts are sold to hospitals for transplanting organs.

The extensive use of the death penalty and the severity of punishments in China and in many other dictatorships, are unacceptable by western standards, but before we start to feel smug, we should recall that only 70 years ago the German state, Hitler's Third Reich, executed six millions Jews and others for no other "crime" than race. There is a relationship between dictatorship and the severity of punishment for crimes against the state. Conversely, the more democratic the state, the more lenient the punishments are likely to be.

The relationship between punishment and time is a clear one. Indeed, the term "doing time" means spending time in prison. Community service penalties imposed by the courts specify the number of hours or days. In schools, detention for a specified amount of time after the school day is still a common punishment.

Historically, there used to be a relationship between punishment and the energy demanded from the offender. Hard labour was a standard form of punishment and still is found in some countries. Thus the relationship between crime and punishment on the one hand and time and energy on the other was recognised. Capital punishment, the extreme penalty, represents the confiscation of the offender's entire stock of time and energy simultaneously.

Corporal punishment as form of punishment has been largely abandoned in the civilised western world. In the UK there has been a major change against it. Fifty years ago the use of the cane was still common in boys' schools with prefects being permitted to use it on smaller boys. This is no longer the case.

The deliberate infliction of pain or torture is still prevalent in most African and Arab nations. In its fight against Islamic extremists the West has been guilty of "rendition": handing suspects over to regimes for which torture is a routine method of dealing with opponents of the state. Many consider that any evidence obtained under torture should not be admissible in law in any circumstances. Far more resources should devoted to finding reliable lie-detecting equipment or, better still, a truth drug that leaves the recipient willing to tell the truth.

The biological purpose of pain is to ensure the survival of the creature concerned. A child learns to avoid touching hot things. Animals quickly learn which of their actions bring pain. Pain was intended by nature to be a warning signal that saved the creature from destruction. Conversely pleasure, for example eating, ensured its survival. The infliction of pain as punishment is almost unique to the human species. When a cat plays with a mouse this is one possible exception. Animals may fight for territory or for access to females but commonly the loser runs away rather than be killed.

The legal infliction of serious cruelty on animals for human gratification in the west is now limited to the barbaric Spanish sport of bull fighting. The bull is tortured by the picadors before being killed by the matador. The picadors' horses frequently are gored by the bull. This so-called sport has now been banned in Spain's Catalonia province.

The use of the whip by jockeys in horse-racing is impossible to justify. If none carried whips the horses might run slower but would be spared undeserved punishment. In the UK the racing authorities have now limited the number of strokes that a jockey may inflict to eight in jump races and seven on the flat. Banning the whip completely would place more emphasis on the jockeys' skills rather than their cruelty.

Hunting of foxes, deer and hares with dogs was finally banned in the UK in 2004. The sport was particularly cruel in the case of deer who died by being torn to death over several minutes rather than almost at once in the case of foxes and hares. Hunting was the preserve of land-owning gentry who traditionally support the Conservative Party. Had David Cameron won an outright majority in 2010 he might have brought back hunting in order to please his backwoodsmen, but mercifully he was unable to do so as the Liberal Democrats, his coalition partners, would never have supported him.

Some societies or units within societies historically used pain as punishment in order to protect that society's survival. Painful punishment was standard in the world's navies in the nineteenth century. Ships held public floggings for minor offences. In some navies each ship had a member of the company designated as a flogging-master, so frequent was the use of flogging. Within the customs of the time, such brutal punishment was accepted as normal.

Dogs and cats usually respond to their owners' voices and recognise anger when they have offended. It seems likely that rewarding good behaviour is more effective than inflicting pain. Mother cats occasionally cuff their kittens when the latter become obstreperous but this corporal punishment is mild by comparison with the slaps and worse inflicted by some humans on their children. It seems that the infliction of pain for punishment is yet another of the less than endearing characteristics of the human race that place us below the animal kingdom in terms of "humanity".

Corruption and transparency

The word 'corrupt' is commonly used, and misused, to describe societies, organisations, activities and individuals. Corruption is generally against the law but in many countries it is so widespread that it is seen as part of the system instead of being outside it. Because the word is used so much, a definition may be helpful. Mine is as follows:

-   corruption occurs when an individual covertly receives payment in money or benefits in order to influence an action for which he has authority.[9]

A feature of corruption is that it is usually hidden by the corrupt person. However, in some countries, notably the Gulf and African states and in others such as Indonesia, corruption is institutionalised. Firms bidding for public contracts in these countries know that they must pay about 10 per cent of the contract to the politicians or functionaries awarding it. It is said that in Indonesia the appropriate bribe however is shared downwards in the ministry or agency concerned according to grade and is seen as a legitimate perk like tips given to waiters. Even in industrialised countries, corruption has been endemic among politicians but is still considered to be wrong. Russia has corruption deeply embedded in its structure of industry and government and the resulting billionaires buy football teams.

---

[9] For a full discussion of defining corruption see Ian Senior, *Corruption: the world's big C.* Institute of Economic Affairs 2006

Transparency backed by significant penalties for offenders is widely seen as the best safeguard against corruption. Politicians in the UK are required to declare their financial interests when they take office and ministers must divest themselves of financial interests that could produce conflicts of interest. Nevertheless there still are periodic "cash-for-questions" scandals and commonly these give rise to resignations.

Corruption, as defined above, does not include fiddling expenses which was rife in the British parliament in under Tony Blair and then Gordon Brown. Fiddling expenses is simply a form of white-collar theft and should be dealt with as such. A handful of British MPs and lords went to prison for very short terms for fiddling expenses while others quickly handed back some of what they had stolen and were given jobs in David Cameron's government.

Within the concept of the three dimensions of man — economic, spiritual and sexual — it is clear that economic man is potentially the most corruptible. An individual who is high on the economic scale is more likely to take dishonest or corrupt actions.

Spiritual man is not concerned with wealth. The spiritual dimension in an individual does not need claims on other people's time and energy to function. Of course his economic dimension does, and if he wishes to convert ideas conceived by the mind into action, he then must use his own time and energy or else have claims on those of others in the form of money. That said, it is hard to imagine a person who is high on the spiritual dimension being corruptible. I cannot imagine that Mother Theresa of Calcutta would have taken covert bribes.

Sexual man may be corruptible. It is said that in some countries it is common to supply a pretty girl to the hotel rooms of a businessmen on buying missions. Foreign male diplomats in Russia are warned not to let themselves be seduced by female under-cover KGB officers. That said, the bribes used for corruption are generally money or assets whose value far exceed the cost of a call-girl.

I conclude that economic man is the cause of corruption and crime in society. Crime used to be thought of as a symptom of a poor society in which the 'have-nots' were criminals who preyed upon the 'haves'. The assumption was that if there was more wealth to be shared in the society in question and it was distributed under a democratic system in ways which were seen as fair, crime would wither. Experience in the west does not support this simplistic view. Further, Russia and other former socialist countries where democracy was implanted in the 1990s, crimes of every sort including corruption are high and rising.

There are various explanations of why this is happening. First, the penalties for many crimes, and certainly economic crime, were more severe under the former socialist regimes. Moreover, the ostensible differences in wealth between the rich and poor were less extreme under socialism than they have become under the hastily introduced market economies.

Crime and corruption are viruses: once they have entered a society, they can be eradicated only if those at the very top wish to do so. In the USA, for example, there was no prospect of corruption being tackled by a president such as Richard Nixon who was willing to authorise burglary of his political opponents and to use public funds to have his private residence improved.

What kinds of punishment are just?

Once a society has defined certain actions as crimes it must impose penalties on those who commit them. As noted, the concepts of what constitutes a crime and what are appropriate punishments vary over time between nations and cultures and indeed between judges and other law enforcers in a given jurisdiction. Before sentencing an offender it is normal for a judge to call for reports on the person's background. Thus the offence in itself is not seen as an absolute requiring an absolute punishment. Generally, only offences that are routine and minor receive an inflexible punishment such as a parking fine. There are significant variations in the punishments awarded by different judges for a clearly defined offence such as burglary, with some judges sentencing offenders to several years in prison while others are released on probation.

All would agree that there must be some relationship between the gravity of a crime and the severity of the punishment but how can we find a rational way to make the punishment fit the crime? Consider theft, for example. A person who steals a car takes an asset with a specific market value. That value, in monetary terms, reflects the accumulation of time and energy required to transform materials and to put the car on the road. Let us say that the car is worth 1000 Roines. The thief has taken possession of something worth 1000 Roines and given nothing in return. If he is caught, what would be a fair sentence?

In the first place he should return the car to its owner. If it has been damaged he should pay in Roines the cost of the repair. If the car has been sold or written off, he should pay to the owner the car's full value and any expenses the latter may have incurred in hiring another car. To this should be added compensation for lost time resulting from the car's theft. Next he should pay a fine to the state for the time taken by the police in bringing him to justice and to the court in trying him. Thus a correct punishment would make the offender repay in Roines the full costs incurred by all the parties affected by the theft.

In practice, the judicial system does otherwise. The person whose car has been stolen claims against his insurance. The offender may pay a fine that goes to the state and bears no relation to the cost of catching and trying him. Alternatively he may go to prison as a punishment which brings no economic benefit to the person whose car was stolen but rather places a significant financial burden on tax-payers.

In a correctly working system, the thief would go to prison only if he was unable to compensate in Roines all those involved in the case. The purpose of prison would be to make loss of freedom combine with training and education so that the offender would not need to steal cars to make a living. If the offender has marketable skills he should be electronically tagged to go to work until his debt to those involved has been paid off. Prison should be about reforming criminals who have no way of repaying their victims and society generally.

Let us now consider the merits and demerits of this system of punishing offenders. The clearest merits are these:

-        offenders make direct restitution to those they have wronged, beginning with the victim and including a wider society;

- sentences have a direct and transparent relationship between the gravity of the offence in terms of Roines, and the sentence passed;

- some offenders will not go to prison. Instead, if tagged they stay at home as productive members of society and have an incentive to pay off their sentence in terms of Roines as quickly as possible; and

- those sent to prison can have day release for their job and continue to be productive members of society while paying off their Roines sentence. Loss of freedom in evenings and at week-ends together with Spartan amenities in prison would be an incentive to make offenders wish to complete their sentences as soon as possible.

Now let us consider one potential criticism. The first is that a given sentence, when denominated in Roines, would take far longer to pay off for an offender with no savings and low-value skills than for a wealthy offender with savings and high value skills. There would seemingly be one law for the rich and one for the poor, because a rich man who stole a car would avoid prison by paying the full penalty in Roines and leave the court a free man. A poor man, however, with no savings and no skills, would have his earnings attached for years because of the time it would take him to earn 1000 Roines. However, he would not be in prison unless he was likely to abscond and thus fail to repay his debt. In simple terms, a rich man could buy his way out of prison; a poor man would have to do time.

This aspect does not invalidate the case. The criminal justice system needs to be based on making criminals compensate their victims and society. Time spent in prison does not represent any form of compensation. Nobody is better off unless the criminal learns from his time in prison and does not re-offend. The coalition government is moving in this direction.

For more serious offences, notably murder, compensation payable in Roines is less appropriate as prison becomes a matter of safeguarding the public from repeat offences. However, compensation to dependents of the murdered victim may be appropriate. For example, a widow whose bread-winning spouse is dead should indeed receive compensation from the murderer to help her bring up the children.

White collar theft
White collar theft is increasing. It ranges from using stolen credit cards at one end of the scale. At the other end we see the raiding of pension funds by Robert Maxwell; systematic financial plundering of the company by executives of Enron and WorldCom in 2002 and by Bernie Madoff's Ponzi investment scheme which collapsed in 2008.

At present there is often a disparity between the prison sentences passed for white-collar theft and what could be called blue-collar theft. A man who steals £1,000 over a post office counter may spend several years in prison. A few MPs who stole thousands by cheating on their expenses were sent to prison for 18 months. One MP, Michael Gove, quickly repaid £7,000 that he had claimed by "flipping" houses and was immediately put into David Cameron's cabinet.

A valid reason for the different degrees of punishment lies in the potential or actual violence entailed in physical, blue-collar robbery as compared with non-violent white collar robbery. Violence in blue-collar crime may impose severe distress on the victims that should certainly be compensated by the criminal. On the other hand, the distress caused to investors or pensioners whose savings have been stolen by white collar criminals may be as severe and long-lasting.

White collar criminals are better educated and have more professional earning capacity than blue-collar criminals. The amounts they take may be of much higher value than the items taken by blue-collar criminals. Of course, there are exceptions in both directions and the distinction between white and blue collar crime is not always clear. Criminals who take famous paintings might be classed as either white or blue-collar.

White collar criminals are more likely to have assets to confiscate for payment to their victims and society. The house and car are two obvious assets. White collar criminals are more likely to find a prison regime uncomfortable by contrast with their normal life-style. This gives them additional motivation to avoid prison and hence to pay for their crimes.

Conclusion

Where well functioning democracies are established crime is countered with proportionate though not always appropriate forms of punishment. Because of the historical trend towards leniency, some criminals escape with light punishments, particularly so if they are of professional background. The length of their sentence is often short and made shorter by remission for good conduct.

Victims sometimes receive compensation from public funds, which is absurd. It is the convicted criminal who should compensate the victim, not the state. Victims of crime should be compensated from state funds only when nobody has been convicted for the crime. In this case, the state can be seen to be making redress to the victim for the state's failure to provide adequate law, order and policing.

In essence, all economic crime, whether blue collar or white, is carried out by economic man and is based on stealing assets that represent capitalised time and energy; or money that represents claims on other people's assets and services. A system of punishments which makes criminals repay their victims and society in terms of time and energy would be fair and transparent. It would eliminate arbitrary sentences by eccentric judges and above all it would be humane. Such a system, however novel it seems, has clear advantages that would make it worth implementing.

Ian Senior: *Time and Energy*

24   PACKAGING AND LITTER

This chapter may well seem to be about rather trivial matters yet its purpose is to show how the principle of time and energy underlies even small aspects of everyday life.

Packaging is a hall-mark of the industrialised world.   In poor societies many consumer goods, notably food, are sold unpackaged. The farmer picks fruit from his trees, takes it to market, puts it on display, and sells it to the consumer. In industrialised societies the fruit is picked, cleaned, sometimes cooked and then packaged in glass, tin, plastic or paper. These days most consumer goods are packaged in some way except some fresh vegetables. Even cheap items such a nails and screws now come in little plastic boxes hanging conveniently on hooks in DIY stores. The days of the traditional ironmonger are long since gone.

The nature of packaging varies with the item concerned but a primary aim is to save the time and energy of the final user. Consider nails and screws. The customer saves time because having found the size he wants, no shop assistant has to weigh, count or package them and he saves time at the check-out counter.

Much packaging is intended to protect the goods while in transit and to ensure that they reach the consumer in perfect condition. Thus, the packaging of cornflakes needs to be of semi-rigid cardboard to prevent them being crushed. How does a cornflakes packet represent a saving of time and energy given that the cardboard concerned requires time and energy to produce?

By protecting the product it ensures that it is not wasted through damage. The western consumer, brought up in a world in which supply always exceeds demand, is choosy. Damaged goods are rejected and have sharply reduced or no value. Thus, the manufacturer learns that the cost of not providing packaging exceeds the cost of doing so.

Most aspects of modern packaging are designed to save the user's time and energy. Cartons of milk and detergent have tabs and perforations so that they can be opened without using scissors or a knife. Many now have screw tops. Wine bottles increasingly have screw tops which are much easier to open than traditional corks. Screw tops for jam undo with one quarter of a turn whereas a few years ago three or four turns were needed. The age of aerosols for furniture polish and other uses was brought in because less effort was needed to press the aerosol spray than to take a traditional tin of furniture polish, open it, wipe the polish and close the tin after use. Washing powder comes with scoops to save time in measuring what you use. Soup is packaged to suit the number of servings you may want. Everything is done to save time and energy for the wholesaler, retailer and user.

Hygiene plays an important role in packaging anything that is eaten or drunk yet hygiene itself is an aspect of time and energy. If I consume dirty food and am unwell, I lose energy and am forced to spend time in ways I do not choose. Therefore I prefer to buy food or take medicines that have been packaged to ensure their hygiene. The manufacturer knows this and designs his packaging to ensure that I do not get sick from his product.

The physical resources consumed by the packaging industry have become a matter of concern in a world which is increasingly environmentally conscious. Laws exist in developed countries to ensure that a substantial part of packaging is recycled. Some of the most glaringly wasteful forms of packaging are now being recycled, for example drinks canisters and glass bottles.

Packaging has no intrinsic value to the consumer once it has served its purpose of delivering the contents in perfect condition. After that it is regarded as waste. A set of advertisements proclaimed "you are what you junk". The advertisers went through the dustbins of some famous people looking for empty bottles of their own brand of beer. In all western societies large areas of land are filled in with society's industrial and consumer waste. The land used thus is blighted. It cannot be built on because the waste does not provide firm foundations. It cannot be used for agriculture because consumer waste has toxic content.

Burning packaging and other forms of industrial and consumer waste has the merit of enabling its energy to be used once more, but it is only a partial solution that does not constitute recycling.

Litter is a particularly unpleasant way of dealing with waste but reflects the predictable actions of economic man. Economic man drinks beer from a can in a country lane. The empty can has no further value to him. To carry it home requires energy (however minute in relation to the act of walking). To find a litter-bin requires time and energy. To drop the can in the country lane requires neither time nor energy. Actually it imposes on someone else the task of picking up the can, finding a litterbin or taking it home. So economic man (who by his nature is concerned only with economising his personal time and energy) thinks nothing of throwing the beer can into the hedge. At an industrial level, economic man thinks nothing of pumping his waste material into the atmosphere, a river or the sea unless he is constrained from doing so by regulations enforced by fines or other penalties.

Economic man can be constrained from littering and in some countries is so with conspicuous success. In Singapore — probably, along with Switzerland, the cleanest country in the world — substantial on-the-spot fines are imposed for littering and chewing-gum is banned. In other industrialised countries there are fines for littering, but not on-the-spot. Further, these fines are no deterrent to solitary beer-drinkers in country lanes.

I suggest a solution to the litter problem which would harness the natural inclinations of economic man. Instead of fining people who drop litter and are seldom caught, the solution is to reward everyone who picks it up. Each package of a fast-moving consumer good should be valued at a single sum, say one Roine or 10p. A regulation would be passed that any person who handed one package to a retailer of the product concerned would be paid one Roine. This would be printed on the package. Immediately litter in the streets and countryside would have a cash value when picked up and handed in.

Under my system a tobacconist would be compelled under law to pay one Roine in cash for each cigarette pack returned. He would return the pack to the wholesaler who would pay him one Roine. The wholesaler would pass the pack to the cigarette maker and would receive one Roine. At the end of the chain of transactions, the manufacturer would have the package back for recycling which is precisely what environmentalism requires, and the streets would be free of litter.

What objections could there be to this scheme? The most obvious is that the value to the manufacturer of the package, even when recycled, might be less than one Roine. However, this would not present a problem. Initially he would be out of pocket as all the packs outside his factory gate came back for recycling under the scheme. He would have paid for them on their return and having recycled them might still be out of pocket. He would therefore need to increase the price of his product to make up loss. This increase would pass down the distribution chain and be paid by the consumer. However, there would be a saving in the costs of municipal cleaning services.

The scheme has the attraction that the cost of recycling packaging and of dealing with litter would fall indirectly on those who drop the litter. Thus smokers would find that the cost of cigarettes would increase because of the refund payable by the original manufacturer to the people who handed in empty packs. Litterers rather than society in general would pay for littering. Once the system was working, the Roine charged on each packaged article would act like a deposit, ensuring that the packaging was continually recycled.

At its simplest, a manufacturer would add one Roine to the product's price. This additional Roine would pass down the distribution chain to the consumer who, just once, would pay one Roine more for the packaged product. From then on, having smoked the cigarettes or drunk the beer, he could return the pack when buying the next one.

Thus, only for a short period would he be out of pocket and, in future, provided he returned the used pack, the goods concerned would revert in real terms to their previous price. If he did not return the pack he would effectively be fined on the spot! If he put the pack in his own dust-bin he would have made a conscious choice not to recycle the product and would effectively pay a fine. If he littered by throwing the pack into the hedgerow his next beer or packet of cigarettes would cost him an additional Roine. Someone else would readily earn a Roine for recycling the package.

The scheme would be applied not just consumer packaging but equally to industrial packaging. Crates, pallets, sacks and canisters of every kind would have a Roine value attached to them, ensuring that they were returned to the manufacturer. It might not be necessary to return them overseas. For example, in the case of an industrial metal box the importer in the country concerned would receive empty cartons, pay the deposits and sell the metal to the local recycling plant at the going rate. Whatever net loss he made on these transactions would be passed on to customers in the form of higher prices, as with consumer goods.

Would the scheme be universally applicable to industrial waste? No: there would still be a need to control pollution of air, sea and land by products which cannot be recovered. This is already the case. In industrial economies emissions are already regulated and enforced with deterrent fines or tradable carbon permits. These are a market-based way to encourage manufacturers to reduce their carbon emissions. Scientific advance is making it easier to identify polluters. It is now possible to identify the "genetic finger-print" of oil, to say which well it came from and to say which factory is sending a given waste emission into the atmosphere. All that is needed is the political will to reduce industrial pollution.

If one country sets higher environmental standards than others, its manufacturers are at a disadvantage. They must install extra equipment that from the customer's point of view does not show up in the finished product's value. Yet the customers themselves can support and reinforce environmental consciousness in producers. More and more consumer packaging is labelled as made of recycled material. Spiritual man can influence economic man to some extent, even in purely economic transactions.

There will never be an industrialised society without packaging, but there can be a world without litter and unnecessary industrial pollution. Solutions based on an understanding of time and energy are more likely to succeed than others.

25   THE CREATIVE ARTS

The creative arts are the highest form of man's expression. The creative urge in men and women is driven, I believe, mainly by spiritual man but nevertheless economic and sexual man have a role to play. Mozart, Shakespeare and Molière all produced their work because they needed money to live by. Thus they used their imaginative and creative talents in exchange for a claim on the goods and services of others for life's necessities.

Perhaps a truly creative person is willing to create without caring whether his creation will be seen, heard or appreciated by others. Such people are few. Most people, when they create, hope to hear applause, to receive acclaim, preferably now and less preferably in posterity. Present acclaim in the arts can lead to the stupendous fame and fortune that a pop singer or film star can achieve. Acclaim in a more esoteric art form such as poetry can lead to a modest livelihood. Acclaim in any form nourishes spiritual man to create further.

The role of economic man in creation is to convince the spiritual man in him that his creative output will produce claims on goods, services and energy that economic man needs. Therefore the voice of economic man speaks to the artist labouring unrecognised in his garret. His economic voice tells him that he could avoid being hungry if he did a conventional job. His spiritual voice answers back that the world's acclaim will bring good things in plenty and spiritual satisfaction as well.

The role of sexual man in the creative arts is spasmodic. Occasionally he inspires spiritual man to write love poetry or to paint wonderful pictures of his muse. Throughout ages the beauty of the female body has been an inspiration to many. Possibly a few pop songs dealing with love are genuinely inspired by that emotion but more commonly the topic of love is just a suitable subject for a song in the same way that the weather is a suitable subject for conversation between strangers in a bus.

The output of the creative artists and their art is part of the market in capitalised energy but it has some major peculiarities. The time and energy required by Picasso to paint canvases may have been the same as for other artists yet the monetary value placed on Picasso's paintings became legendary in his lifetime.

The starting point is to understand that Picasso, like every other economic person, was initially setting out to add value to the painting materials. Because many people wanted to possess his paintings, those who were prepared to pay most were able to obtain them. Although Picasso was prolific, supply of his paintings was finite. For the market to clear, the price of his paintings went up.

To begin with we must suppose that spiritual men, looking at Picasso's work, valued it for the artistic satisfaction it gave them. Before long, however, economic man recognised that the paintings were acquiring a store of unearned value because their price was rising faster than prices generally. So Picassos and some other forms of art came to be prized by economic man not just for their artistic merit but as a good store of value and often a better one than real estate or stocks and shares.

Yet a Picasso has no intrinsic value as a store of energy. The art market like all markets, is volatile, though less so than stock exchanges. Thirty years from now Picasso may be out of fashion and his paintings of little value; or their value may have continued to soar.

The parallel between Picasso's paintings and paper money extends to considerations of reproduction and forgery. Undetected forged paintings acquire a value to the forger and to subsequent owners equivalent to the genuine article. Thus, the claims a forger can make on other goods, services or forms of energy are the same as though the painting is real, just as a forged bank note, while undetected, can be exchanged for the same goods, services and energy as a real note. It is therefore clear that governments, who are the issuers of paper money, and the artists themselves during their lifetimes, have a strong interest in preventing forgeries. Governments, who print money without having earned it, as many do these days, take exception to allowing others the same right. In olden days forgers were executed.

Forgers of Picassos are not executed but can be pursued in the courts, fined and imprisoned. Legislators, who being politicians are highly economic, usually decide that the value of an artist's creations must not be fraudulently taken from him by forgers. In the same way, the value of paper currencies and stocks and shares depends on confidence that the pieces of paper represent genuine claims on goods, services and energy, and they must therefore be protected by the law.

In addition to penalties for forgery, most societies impose penalties for unauthorised copying. In this case the motives of economic man in imposing rules to protect intellectual property are much the same as those for forgery. For creations to be forthcoming in the first place, spiritual man has to eat. Once he has produced a creation such as a song or a painting, modern technologies can reproduce it perfectly as many times as wanted. If the creator receives no royalties he has less incentive to create. It may have been a blessing to the world, though not to Mozart, that he was continually in need of money. Had his early work earned him the kind or royalties that Andrew Lloyd-Webber earns from one song today, Mozart's output might have been limited to a handful of works.

In developing countries the enforcement of patents and copyright protection is generally negligible. So too is the quantity and quality of creative output. Here again we see the market at work. In developing countries people have few resources to spend on building concert halls, art galleries and theatres, and the public has little money to spend going to events in them. So, although much creative talent may exist waiting to be tapped, it begins to flower only when economic man's primary needs of food, clothing, shelter and education have been satisfied. The protection of spiritual man's creative gifts by economic man for economic reasons is a case in which the interests of both coincide.

The relationship between economic progress and the protection of creations of the mind, namely intellectual property, is seen in Japan. After the Second World War Japanese products were excellent copies devoid of creativity. As Japan's industry advanced, so copying waned, and now in fields as different as cars, cameras and microwave cookers, Japanese products incorporate creativity protected by national and international law. The rapidly industrialising countries of south-east Asia, notably Indonesia, Malaysia, Thailand and Hong Kong are all in the process of putting an end to the pirating of creations, whether artistic or industrial.

Of all the creative arts, music is the most spiritual. The medium for musical creation is the most universal instrument of all, the human voice. The less that creative art depends on matter as its medium, the easier it is to copy or pirate. Songs can be pirated instantly. A Picasso may take some days or weeks to forge. I am unaware of any attempts to forge Henry Moore's large sculptures. When these get stolen, it is for the value of the metal in them.

It can therefore be seen that the more current or capital energy it takes to copy an artistic creation, the less likely it is to be forged. On the other hand, the greater the value that can be attached to an original, the greater the incentive to forge or copy.

The position of poetry as a form of creative art is curious. Few poets make more than the simplest living from writing professionally. Why is poetry so little valued by spiritual and economic man? I suggest that words are so rooted in everyday life that for most people, most of the time, they have little magic. Music, by contrast, has almost no practical application beyond helping soldiers to march in step and aerobic classes to keep to a rhythm. Yet music in all its multitude of sounds and rhythms appeals to every human being and indeed it is now used as music therapy for children with learning disabilities. The existence of this universal appeal proves that all humans have a spiritual dimension.

There is a market for the creative arts just as there is for every other form of output. In that market poetry appeals to a minority and generally commands far less value than other artistic creations. As a claim on other resources therefore the value of poetry is slight. By contrast, Picasso's suppliers, I believe, sometimes did not cash his cheques because they believed that the signature was of more value than the monetary value of the cheque.

The brand Shakespeare commands value. Even some of his most banal plays are performed just because they are his. Yet it is likely that the total box office takings this century from the performances of the world's greatest poet fall well below the royalties from Irving Berlin's *White Christmas* or a song from Lloyd-Webber's *Phantom of the Opera*.

26 MIGRATION

From earliest times man has travelled. Until the 20th century travel
was slow. In previous centuries it was arduous and sometimes
dangerous. The rich rode on horseback or in carriages, the poor went
on foot. Sea voyages were perilous and uncomfortable.

The steam engine changed all that. Steam ships could go where they
wanted when they wanted and steam provided heat for passengers as
well. The steam train reduced travel time compared with coaches,
increased comfort and reliability and brought cheap travel to the
masses. The modern era of mass air travel began in the 1960s and
changed the concept of travel from necessity to fun. Tourism became
big business.

Migration, however, is not to be confused with tourism. People who
take overseas holidays do so for pleasure. Those who migrate do so
mainly for economic reasons. A few people migrate for spiritual
reasons. Centres of learning, culture or religion throughout the ages
have attracted people to move from one city to another or one
country to another. Occasionally people migrate for sexual reasons,
notably marriage.

As a rule most people, most of the time, prefer not to migrate.
Gipsies, Irish travellers and a few nomadic tribes appear to be
exceptions that are discussed below.

What brings about migration? The most important causes are desire
for:
-        a better standard of living;

- better climate;
- freedom from repression; or
- war.

Apart from the insecurity of war, the first three causes of migration have one underlying cause: *the desire to obtain more net energy in a given amount of time.* Migration in fact reflects the working of the theory. Let us take the first three causes in turn.

The desire for a *better standard of living* is a quest for the possibility to obtain more net energy in a given amount of time. A worker migrates from Mexico to the USA because, for doing the same job, he receives two or three times more claims on other forms of energy than in Mexico, notably food, housing and transport. Where people see wealth to be made, there they migrate.

Migration for *a better climate* does not just mean old people retiring to Bournemouth or Spain. Throughout history economic man has found that better climates enabled his acquisition of net energy to be increased. In the simplest case, farming in a good climate produces more food than in a bad one, so economic man moved to climate-friendly areas of the globe. For one man-hour of time he could obtain more food from tilling the soil in a good climate than a bad. In just the same way, modern nomads move their flocks always seeking new and better pastures so that the animals grow fat quicker. Thus they become a store of energy to be consumed directly as meat or indirectly following their exchange for other forms of energy.

Economic man moves to *worse* climates only if by doing so he obtains significantly larger claims on other goods, services or energy to compensate for putting up with the worse climate. Thus high salaries attract people to work in the Gulf States and Alaska. As individuals, they do not migrate permanently because once they have made enough money they return to better climates. Nevertheless, so long as the countries with bad climates can go on providing higher net energy, migration takes place.

Examples of modern migration to bad climates are found in the Gulf States. These are serviced by cheap migrant labour from countries such as the Philippines, India, Pakistan and by expensive skilled labour from the west. The Gulf States have little indigenous population, few skills and little taste for work. However, most have abundant capital energy, namely oil and gas. By selling capital energy they obtain the personal energy of migrant labour. As soon as the oil runs out, the migrants will return from the Gulf to better climates, the Bentleys will rust in the desert, shiny buildings will stand empty and Riyadh, Jeddah, Kuwait, Abu Dhabi, Dubai and others will become ghost towns.

The third cause of migration — freedom from repression — also has its main cause in the quest for energy, though less obviously so. Historically, spiritual man has migrated when he was not free to practise his particular form of religion. The Pilgrim Fathers and the Huguenots were such cases. However, it is clear that the numbers who have migrated on purely spiritual grounds in the past and today can be counted in thousands, while those who have migrated on economic grounds can be counted in millions. Indeed, a continuing problem in wealthy countries is to prevent illegal immigration. Probably 11 million or 3.5 per cent of the US population are illegal immigrants.

The relationship between migration for economic and for spiritual reasons is this. The regimes which restrict spiritual freedom are those that also restrict economic freedom. The heavy hand of communism and Islam are clear examples. Economic man continually tries to increase the net energy he can acquire in a given amount of his time. Communism and indeed all dictatorships whether of the far left or right all constrain economic man on how he acquires and how he uses his personal energy. During the Chinese "cultural revolution" millions were forced to use their personal energy as manual labourers in the fields. In Cambodia the unspeakable Khmer Rouge leader Pol Pot, in the name of socialism, introduced forced labour coupled with mass extermination, sending a million or more of his fellow countrymen to the killing fields, an achievement to rank him in the 20th century's hall of infamy along with Hitler and Stalin.

History shows clearly that the vast bulk of migration represents the movement of economic man in his quest for more net energy and this will continue to be so. By contrast, spiritual man migrates relatively little providing that he is allowed to do and be what he wants without interference.

Migration by sexual man is not an issue except in attempts to gain citizenship through marriage or to bring family members into the country.

From earliest times migration has caused antagonism between existing inhabitants and migrants. Riots and killings occur over land, housing and jobs. In recent years there have been race riots and minor ethnic wars in countries as diverse as the USA, the former member states of the Soviet Union, the Middle East, France, England, Belgium, Sweden, South Africa, India, Pakistan and Sri Lanka. In general, the more clearly differentiated are the migrants, the more the antagonism. For this reason, black and brown minorities in white countries are particularly prone to be the focus of violence.

Even migrants who have no obvious ethnic differences cause antagonism and violence. The interminable troubles of Northern Ireland result from migration from Britain two centuries earlier. Protestants and Catholics look identical and only subtle distinctions exist in such things as their names, speech and the schools they went to. Yet these distinctions, given expression in the branch of Christianity which they happen to have been born into, remain the reason why during the Troubles about 3,000 were murdered with primitive abandon. The bitter wars between Serbs, Croatians and Muslims in the former Yugoslavia date back to migration from the Middle Ages onwards.

The prospects for antagonism and violence are in direct relationship to
- the speed and volume of the influx of migrants;
- the extent to which immigrants threaten to take over existing assets, notably land, housing and jobs; and
- the degree to which there are obvious differences in appearance and behaviour compared with the existing population.

Throughout the world governments have recognised that migration causes strains on societies and therefore the movement of people, both permanent and temporary, is controlled by passports and other regulations.

A less common reason for limiting free migration is because in some cases migration is a brain drain or skill drain. The state, through taxation, invests time and energy in training its citizens. These acquire human capital which has been paid for by others. With justification, governments in some countries do not allow human capital paid for by taxes to emigrate freely.

Migration represents a loss of investment by the source country and a corresponding gain by the recipient country. The resources required to train a doctor are substantial. When a doctor migrates, he takes with him the benefit of his training. Using the skills he has been taught he expects to earn a larger yield of net energy than he would have without the training. Therefore, the expenditure of public time and energy produces private gain. If the doctor practises in the country where he was trained, he repays his debt to his fellow citizens. For example, junior hospital doctors in the UK work unusually long hours for low wages and thus clearly make a repayment to the state for their training. If the newly qualified doctors migrate they take with them as human capital the proceeds of other people's time and energy.

As discussed earlier, the argument for student loans is based on the above reasoning and in economic terms is evidently just. Migration is driven first and foremost by the quest for net energy. Brain and skill drains are part of this phenomenon. In a world of antipathy towards migrants and increasing violence coupled with the cheapness of travel, economic man's natural tendency to migrate in search of more net energy needs to be constrained. Since history shows that it takes decades or generations for migrants to be assimilated, it follows that migration must be allowed to happen only at the speed that migrants can be absorbed without causing friction within their host society. If too much migration happens too quickly, the migrant groups retain their languages, dress and customs and become enclaves within the host society instead of being absorbed into it. Tensions develop which are kept in check by legal systems if these are non-racist and enforceable. However, at times of economic hardship tensions erupt into sporadic violence against migrant groups. This has occurred in the UK and has caused many indigenous citizens to consider the policies of past governments to create a "muti-cultural" society to be a failure.

The countries of the world where high net energy can be obtained through natural resources or climate will always be targets for economic immigration. Countries with low net energy per head and/or unpleasant climates will always be prone to emigration. Migration controls will be needed for many years in order to prevent the friction and violence that unrestrained migration by economic man causes.

27   WARFARE

Human males naturally possess latent physical violence; human females much less so. A likely explanation lies in the historical role of the two sexes. Man, the hunter, found food which is the basis of energy and hence of survival, while woman, the mother, produced and reared children. The human male, therefore, for many thousands of years has been concerned with seeking food and land. In the past he fought over disputed land and land today is still the prime cause of international conflict.

Warfare makes huge demands on the societies involved. The energy squandered by explosives is immense. The toys of war - battleships, planes, submarines, tanks and missiles - are enormously intensive of time in designing them and energy in building them. The steel in a battleship and a tank derives from the application of heat to ore, energy in rolling the steel, and fuel oil to propel the finished machine. Unlike civil aircraft, warplanes are built with no regard to the energy needed to make them fly except to the extent that the distances they can fly without refuelling affect their performance as weapons of destruction.

Since time immemorial men have fought and killed each other. Animals also fight, particularly in the mating season, until one of them runs. Seemingly man is the only animal which habitually fights to the death. Some fights concern two men only — women seldom fight physically — but much more commonly fighting concerns groups of men. Historically, armies have become much larger over time. In the Middle Ages pitched battles concerned a few thousand men on either side and were finished in hours even though the war itself might drag on for years. The 20th century saw two world wars and innumerable smaller ones. The most spectacular of recent wars in which the west was directly involved was the ejection of Iraqi forces from Kuwait in 1991, the invasion of Afghanistan in 2001 and the toppling of Saddam Hussein in 2003.

In the industrialised world vast resources of time, energy and creativity are devoted to discovering more sophisticated ways of killing and destruction. Modern weapons require fewer combatants and many combatants are nowhere near a traditional battlefield. Some fly bombers, some stand by to operate missiles from silos in distant countries and others are in submarines. The depersonalisation of killing heightens the danger that weapons of mass destruction will be used. It is easier to pull a trigger or launch a missile against unseen people a long way off. This is exemplified in attacks on Al Qaida in Pakistan by drones piloted remotely in the USA.

Meanwhile, in less developed countries traditional combat with aircraft, tanks, artillery and infantry remains the norm. The seven year war between Iraq and Iran was notable for the number of ground based troops killed. The civil war in Syria has so far entailed mainly traditional weapons and gas has been used only briefly.

How does the theory of time and energy explain warfare? First, economic man is the mainspring behind conflict. The primeval need for land has been the driving force for wars throughout history. Economic man fought either to gain new land or to protect what he already had. Land historically was the source of energy and hence wealth. Hitler's war was patently about land as seen in his annexation of Austria and Poland and his occupation of France, Belgium and the

Netherlands. The Israeli-Arab wars have all been about land.

Since oil is now the primary source of wealth it is unsurprising that 1991 should see the most spectacular energy war ever. Iraq's stated reason for invading Kuwait was that Kuwait was lifting quantities of crude oil from fields which ran under the land of both countries. Iraq's historical claim to Kuwait was weak but the attraction of Kuwait's oil-fields was overwhelming.

The intervention of the western allies was not about democracy. The Kuwaiti regime comprised a royal family whose members provided all the ministers and business connections. It was devoid of democracy, vastly rich, paternalistic, corrupt by western standards and not commendable in any obvious way. If Kuwait had been without oil, Saddam Hussein would have been little interested in invading and the west even less interested in ejecting him.

The west engaged in the war because Saddam Hussein had to be driven out of Kuwait to stop him taking the other Gulf states, many of them rich in oil: Saudi Arabia, Bahrain, Qatar and the United Arab Emirates. In conquering them, which would have been easy, Hussein would have controlled about one half of the world's oil and gas supplies. Saddam Hussein would have had the delighted support of the rest of the Muslim world. The ugly face of Islamic fundamentalism would have achieved new legitimacy. The Iraqi empire would have had space, immense energy reserves, a common language, Arabic, and a common religion, Islam. Within little time it would also have had nuclear weapons to add to its arsenal of biological and chemical warheads.

The short, decisive and brilliantly executed operation Desert Storm drove Saddam Hussein's troops out of Kuwait with heavy cost to equipment and loss of some thousands of Iraqi soldiers. Hussein's riposte was to leave the oil wells burning and oil valves pouring crude oil into the sea. History will remember him.

There have been other energy wars in recent years. When part of Nigeria attempted to secede in 1967 under the name of Biafra, the federal Nigerian government knew that Biafra would take with it the country's oil wells. The determination of Britain to keep the Falkland Islands has also been attributed to a belief that the south Atlantic contains oil wells in its coastal waters which could be assured only by a territorial claim to the Falklands.

Territorial possessiveness that produces war is an automatic reflex in economic man which will take centuries to eradicate. However, it does not explain why man kills. That man enjoys violence is evidenced by the regular diet of violence and killings that attract large television and cinema audiences as did the Roman circuses two thousand years ago. It also explains the continuation of bull fighting in Spain and boxing world-wide, unquestionably the world's two most barbaric sports.

My general theory explains why man kills. An enemy who has tried to take my land or otherwise injure me is no longer a threat when he is at my feet begging for mercy, but he may become a threat again if he escapes. To kill him requires little time or energy on my part now. To fight him again at some time in the future will require more time and energy and the outcome is uncertain. Killing him becomes an economic solution.

In the past prisoners of war or wealthy citizens were frequently held as hostages to be exchanged for ransom. Piracy and hostage-taking have become a routine form of livelihood in the failed African state of Somalia.

Do spiritual man and sexual man have any part in warfare? It is tempting to blame the Troubles in Northern Ireland and the civil war in Syria on spiritual man because of the religious affiliations of the two sides but it seems more likely that the protagonists are economic men using the banner of religion to justify basic economic goals.

Sexual man can be entirely exculpated from causing wars. Though he may fight like a stag in rut over a dolly-bird in a bar, no war has been fought for sex since Helen of Troy.

The collapse of the Soviet empire and of socialism in other parts of east Europe brought numerous long-standing ethnic and religious tensions into the open and produced an ethnic war in the former Yugoslavia.

Wars are much more easily waged by dictators. Democracies find that to go to war there must be acceptance by the majority. In democracies the president or prime-minister is commander-in-chief, but mechanisms remain which enable voters and cabinet ministers to remove incompetent leaders in war time.

It is difficult for a democracy to be forced unwillingly into a war by its leaders. Governments require a powerful propaganda machine to do so. Tony Blair, the British Labour prime-minister who took the UK into the war against Iraq in 2003, had a spin machine that relied on two key pieces of misinformation: that Iraq had chemical and biological weapons of mass destruction, which was denied at the time by Hans Blix, the UN's head of the UN's inspection commission; and that rockets with a range of targeting Israel and beyond could be launched within 40 minutes.

Wisdom after the event is perfect and after the invasion of Iraq no such weapons or rockets were found. The only limp excuse that Blair can leave for posterity is that it was better to be safe than sorry in dealing with an unbalanced dictator like Hussein.

Dictators such as the Hitler, Stalin and Saddam Hussein having crushed all democratic opposition were able to wage war whenever it seemed in their interest to do so. By contrast, Israel, which since its foundation has real democracy, has been able to eject prime-ministers and governments throughout years of being spasmodically at war with neighbouring Arab states who deny Israel's right to exist.

Unless ample forms of non-oil energy can be found, the danger of oil wars will increase as oil runs out in aggressive, non-democratic countries. Argentina, when ruled by a military junta, attacked the Falklands in 1982. Today, Argentina still lays vociferous claim to the Falklands but, now enjoying democracy, seems much less likely to attempt to take them again by force.

Primitive man found that it was to his advantage to take his neighbour's land in order to improve his own material wealth, and modern economic man will do the same if not constrained by spiritual man, by democracy or by a new world order enforced by the United Nations.

28   COMPUTERS

The discovery of steam power produced the industrial revolution. Hitherto coal had been used to produce heat only. Through steam, coal became transformed into mechanical energy thus enabling man to accomplish a multitude of things using far less time and personal energy than before. In effect, coal's energy was substituted for man's personal energy.

The discovery of the transistor produced the computer revolution. It substitutes machine thinking for human thinking. A transistor is analogous to a brain cell. Both function with minute electric impulses. Functioning together the brain cells become the intelligence which directs the activities of the body. Transistors become the intelligence that directs the activities of printers, video screens, robots and numerous other forms of machine. Both make extensive use of memory as a place to store information not currently needed and to bring it into use when further instructions are required.

Functioning together, transistors and other components become a computer, a microprocessor or a chip. From the layman's point of view, the words are largely synonymous. The computer directs the functioning of machines as diverse as watches, word-processors, dishwashers, audio and video equipment, robots, telecommunications and broadcasting equipment of all sorts, aircraft, ships, rockets and missiles.

Computers are still in their infancy. Before the invention of transistors, computers were based on slow valves. In the early 1970s an electronic calculator was the size and weight of a large mechanical typewriter and it did just the four basic arithmetic functions. Today, a calculator the size of a credit card can do more functions, runs on solar energy, and costs in real terms perhaps one thousandth of what that calculator cost 40 years ago.

The speed, memory and functions of a computer have continued to advance exponentially while the physical volume needed to house a given level of computing power has shrunk. There is no sign that the curve is about to reach a plateau. Further, the technology for transmitting digital information has become ever faster using fibre-optics and high frequency radio links.

Computers overtook humans 50 years ago in the speed with which they could do simple repetitive tasks. In those days, it was common to liken computers to obedient morons. They had to be shown how to do everything in minutest detail and then they could repeat what they had been taught. People mocked them because they could barely play chess, a game that can be learned by five-year-olds. Today they can do numerous things that people either cannot do or could do only laboriously. The number of applications for computing that mobile telephones can handle continues to increase daily.

In the past ten years computers have overtaken humans in being able to do all the main intellectual activities. Computers can scan and read printed material from the page and recognize voice commands. They have made huge strides in being able to read handwriting but hardly need to do so. Who writes by hand these days when typing on a PC, laptop, tablet or a mobile is so much quicker?

Some of their functions are still clumsy and are not yet commercially viable. Thus, offices are still cleaned by humans rather than by robots. However, on all factory assembly lines, robots have replaced humans and the trend will continue. Robots are quicker, never stop working, and produce work of higher quality.

The state-of-the-art computer today may be equivalent to a five year old child who is one quarter of the way to being fully grown physically and mentally. The advance of computer technology shows no sign of levelling off.

Man's role in developing computers now is to teach them to solve problems he could not possibly solve himself and to make even more powerful computers. In the past, computers could not think for themselves. They could only memorise and repeat sets of instructions, known as programs, which had been fed into them by man. The new generation of computers now works with artificial intelligence. Computers have the power to remember and think akin to man and in many ways can be infinitely more powerful. I can remember 10-20 addresses. A personal computer can remember as many as I care to give it. I can recognise thirty different voices on the telephone without being told the name of the caller. Computers will be able to recognize as many as requested.

A recent discovery with breathtaking implications for society is that every person's blood and body tissues have a DNA "signature" unique to that person that can be reproduced in digital form for computer recognition. Computers, whose powers of recognition and recall are limitless, when equipped with sensors will remember people in their entirety. The modern criminal is photographed but can grow a beard, change his hair style, and in extreme cases undergo plastic surgery. None of these will make a difference to a computer once it has stored his unique DNA signature.

Many people are worried that this rapidly developing technology will give rise to a police state with every detail about every citizen stored in massive central computers as was brilliantly depicted in George Orwell's *1984*. The rights of citizens to have access to data about them have been codified in the UK. However, the rising tide of violence, terrorism and all forms of civil disobedience in western countries will lead inexorably to the creation of central data files in which information about every citizen will be stored according to his DNA signature.

In the war against crime, for example, traditional forensic evidence is frequently inconclusive. A man on a rape charge may be convicted on the basis of identification by a witness who is mistaken, which produces a miscarriage of justice. However, if the victim has even one hair from the assailant, the unique "signature" of the body tissue is sufficient to convict or free the defendant with total certainty. Providing all citizens have access to central records and the right to correct false entries, the law-abiding will have little to fear. Only law-breakers will find that computers are their enemy.

How does the theory of time and energy serve to explain the extraordinarily rapid process in computing design and technology? The computer's prime function is to save time in large degree and, in lesser degree, energy. Taking the computer's most rudimentary function, arithmetic calculation, a pocket calculator can do simple arithmetic say 100 times faster than a human. It can also do logarithms and square roots, which most humans cannot calculate at all and which would take a good mathematician some hours. At a more advanced level, a basic home-computer can recalculate a large table of interrelated formulae in micro-seconds, changing 1,000 figures accurately to 10 decimal places.

At a yet more advanced level, a computer can help to design an aircraft engine or a large building, showing the effects of different assumptions by the draughtsman. On the screen, he can see 10 different versions in minutes. Drawn by hand, each version might take 10 hours or 10 days. The benefit of the computer in all these cases is to make massive savings of human time.

Almost coincidentally, computers also save both human and natural energy. For example, a computer-based distribution system sends the goods vehicles by the shortest, quickest routes. In saving time, they save petrol too. A computer controlled central heating system can monitor the temperature throughout the building and ensure that the boiler is switched off the moment the required temperature is reached.

Telecommunication has become indistinguishable from computing. Telephone exchanges once were full of bulky electro-mechanical equipment. Now the switches are transistor based. The message currents they carry consist of binary digits known as bits. Voice conversations, facsimile messages, computer output, television, video graphics, newspaper pages, a Mozart symphony, all become streams of bits passing along carriers of copper, glass-fibre or radio-wages, and are switched through solid state, digitally controlled computers.

In parallel with the elimination of physical newspapers, letters, books and junk mail are being replaced by laptops and tablets of different sizes on to which a complete novel or a daily newspaper can be downloaded in a matter of seconds. The vast storage areas required by libraries will be needed only for archives of paper-based books that it has been decided are not worth scanning into digital form. Physical publication of huge tomes such as the *Encyclopaedia Britannica* and the *Oxford English Dictionary* ceased a decade ago and their electronic versions have the major advantage of taking up no physical space anywhere and of being perpetually up to date.

The key to the advance of the electronic book has been the development of high resolution, flat screens whose images are as sharp as the printed page and infinitely cheaper to reproduce. The same technology has driven the new generations of flat screen colour television sets which now hang on walls and have a resolution as sharp as a colour photograph. There will be no limit to their size. Broadcasts in 3D are now common and before long will be standard.

The electronic financial world we live in is fragile. Every so often the entire computing system of one of the big banks crashes for a day or more. We must hope that their back-up systems are fool-proof. We can't be sure. But we can be sure that hacking into institutional computing systems is becoming increasing sophisticated. Corporations, banks, government and defence systems are all at risk. Computers are taking over the world and may become out of control.

My theory of time and energy helps us to understand why these things are happening. Progress in civilisation is based upon minimising people's time and energy. Consider, for example, the huge armoured vans needed to move money between banks. They represent large quantities of capitalised energy. The petrol they consume represents current energy. The security staffs who man them represent expenditure of time. All this time and energy can be saved by electronic money transfer which in turn has been made possible by computers.

To many, the thought of paper disappearing as a claim on time and energy seems strange. Yet apart from the dwindling group of people who live solely using cash, paper money has little significance. I am unconcerned whether I have £5 or £50 in my pocket but I am certainly concerned about my bank balance when it appears on a cash dispenser screen or on my PC. And I am very concerned if I cannot access my bank balance to make instant purchases or payments of bills.

A further computer application waiting to be exploited is electronic elections. The USA and Germany for years have used mechanical voting machines. These could become digital and linked to a central computer. When this happens, an entire election result could be known within minutes of the poll closing.

The reason for delay in introducing such a system is the underlying fear that dishonest politicians could rig the system. Politicians in the UK and elsewhere have been found to fiddle their expenses as a matter of routine. Corruption scandals involving senior politicians in most industrialised countries surface often enough for voters to be deeply suspicious of politicians. Staying with the traditional physical ballot paper at present seems the best safeguard that elections are not rigged.

Despite the technical dangers of electronic voting systems being corrupted, there are attractions in giving voters a more immediate say in their affairs. As an intermediate measure, voters could still mark ballot papers but these will then be read electronically and processed by computer. The used ballot papers can be rerun by an independent election auditor to prove the accuracy of the system.

A reason why voting systems are likely to become partly electronic is that they could enable an improvement in democracy. In countries such as Britain and the USA archaic first-past-the-post voting systems have produced monolithic parties and few candidates on the ballot paper. However, those countries with multiple parties and varying systems of proportional representation will benefit from electronic counting systems. Ireland uses the single transferable vote, a system more complex than others but demonstrably fairer to minorities.

Many people who feel uneasy about electronic elections have no qualms about a banking system in which an increasing proportion of transactions are electronic and cheques are on the way out. If I can trust a computer with the complex task of processing 50 transactions monthly in my personal bank account, why should I not trust it with the far simpler task of adding up votes once every few years which I cast for members of parliament and local councillors?

One key question about the future of computers remains. The computer virus was first thought of as a joke. It was said that a payroll clerk many years ago wrote a subroutine into the company's payroll programme so that it would not work if his name was not included on the payroll. Thus he made himself impossible to fire.

Today, the complexity of program writing and the birth of a new activity, "hacking", have led to computer fraud for monetary gain along with computer vandalism for the fun of it. The threat is serious. The contents of a database can be wiped out magnetically in milliseconds. A virus could corrupt some data in small quantities, thus throwing doubt on the entire database's validity and being harder to trace. Cyber warfare has become a reality.

The impetus behind the development of more powerful computers has been the saving of time in analysing complex questions involving huge quantities of data. From the start of the 21st century onwards, when the earth's fossil energy started to run out, the impetus also became the saving of energy. Telecommunication will increasingly be used to enable people to work in their homes instead of commuting to an office. Energy will be devoted to the primary tasks of making and distributing finished goods and the brainpower of computers will be applied to making these activities as economical of energy as possible.

Economic man's perennial desire to save his personal time and energy and his awakening desire to save natural energy will continue to drive the development of super-computers. Like all creations, computers may become a force for good or evil. At present they are a force for good. They represent modest quantities of capital energy and consume small quantities of current energy. In return, they save men untold quantities of time. As servants of economic man, they have served him well to date. However, nuclear wars could be started by a malfunctioning computer and there is increasing concern about the power of governments and others to collect, store and read "big data".

The prospect of computers' future power for good or for evil is daunting. However, attempting to control or stop the advance of computer technology will be like King Canute trying to stop the incoming waves.

29 COURTSHIP, MARRIAGE AND DIVORCE

You might suppose that this chapter would be largely about sexual man yet this is not so. Nevertheless, it is right that we must begin with the sexual urge that ensures the survival of the human race and the animal kingdom.

Most humans at different times in their lives fall in love with or are deeply attracted to another person, generally of the opposite sex. This can occur at an early age and certainly well before puberty. I recall being deeply in love with particular girls when I was seven and then again at 12 and 16. The emotions I felt in the first two cases were passionate, though not particularly sexual. I did not set out to kiss them, nor did I yearn to see them undressed. At 16 and thereafter it was otherwise!

Nature has contrived to make sex immensely enjoyable for most people of both sexes. The extraordinary misunderstanding of women's physiology and sexual needs up to the 1950s led to the belief that only men really enjoyed sex and that the woman's role was to lie back and think of England. Hence the vast numbers of prostitutes who in Victorian days serviced the men whose wives had been brought up to believe that sex was the unpleasant necessity to produce children. An extensive web of taboo, prejudice and Puritanism reinforced the view of women's sexual role. Contraception as we know it now was non-existent. Child bearing was painful and far more dangerous than today. Women had large families which put more stress on their bodies. Many babies died at birth or as children, adding to the emotional strain on mothers. Illegitimacy, particularly in Victorian times and up to the 1960s was seen as a disgrace which branded the woman as an outcast while the man who had impregnated her would probably be excused as sowing wild oats. The entire system in the western world and elsewhere was grossly distorted in favour of male sexuality and against that of women.

Sigmund Freud, the founder of psychotherapy, came to the conclusion that sexual problems were the basis for most mental disorders which in turn produced physiological side-effects. Freud's perceptions of the sexuality of women, and indeed other forms of sexuality, were a product of his age. For example, in one of his cases, that of Little Dora, he refers to "...the perversion which is most repellent to us, the sensual love of a man for a man". He also refers to the sucking of a penis by a woman as "...this excessively repulsive and perverted fantasy". Both practices are now considered to be normal between consenting adults. At least Freud was honest enough to admit that "The uncertainty in regard to the boundaries of what is to be called normal sexual life, when we take different races and different epochs into account, should in itself be enough to cool the zealot's ardour".[10]

The sexual revolution of the swinging 'sixties was largely brought about by the contraceptive pill. Previous methods of contraception involved internal devices used by the woman or condoms used by the man. All had drawbacks and, in the case of women's devices, were unreliable. Abortion was illegal and remains so in catholic countries. Back-street abortion was dangerous, traumatic and was carried out by people without medical training or facilities.

---

[10]   Translated in Sigmund Freud. Volume 8. Case histories I. Penguin Books, p84

The Pill changed all that. Seemingly at a stroke women had been liberated to have sexual partners without taking precautions in advance and the nagging worry of waiting for their next period after the event. Their day of sexual freedom had arrived at last, or so it seemed.

In practice, things were not so simple. Some women found that the Pill produced side-effects. For others, the dramatic change of social perceptions was hard to cope with. For many women sex needs to be associated with much deeper emotional feelings than for men. In a world where women were supposedly free to have sex without worry, pressure increased on them to become as sexually liberated at men wanted. Some men developed the attitude: "I've taken you out to dinner. Now let's go to bed". Some women developed this way of thinking and were able to enjoy what is widely known as recreational sex. Many did not. Thus the imbalance between men and women's sexual needs and aspirations remained. The fact that prostitution, the world's oldest profession, did not close down in the swinging 'sixties is conclusive proof that there were still more men wanting sex than there were women willing to give it, even when on the Pill.

Search for better forms of contraception continued. The two most important inventions were the contraceptive implant, a device that is 99 per cent effective for three years, and the "morning after" pill. Both are a godsend for women who have an unexpected fling and rebelled at carrying condoms in their handbag.

Men's contribution to preventing unwanted pregnancies was the vasectomy. This simple operation can be carried out by a competent general practitioner in his surgery, alone and using a local anaesthetic, in under half an hour. The tiny vessels that carry sperm from the scrotum and mix it with the fluid that he ejaculates, are cut. The surprising result is that his erections and sexual functioning are just as before, but the seminal fluid is devoid of sperm. He is not neutered but infertile. Since the operation is very hard to reverse, it is only for men who are certain that they do not wish to produce more children. In case they may change their minds, some deposit sperm in a sperm bank where it is frozen and can keep for many years for subsequent use if wanted.

The phenomenon of homosexuality in humans is now widely accepted in western society. Pressure groups, frequently known as LGBT (lesbian, gay, bi-sexual and transsexual), start from the assumption that a person's sexuality is in their genes. As Freud and others have pointed out, the ancient Greeks thought homosexuality as normal as heterosexuality. However, for centuries in many western countries it was regarded as perverse, though a number of historical figures were unashamedly gay. Edward II of England had homosexual affairs and was subject to a particularly cruel death. According to Christopher Marlowe's play *Edward the Second*, it was chosen by his enemy Mortimer, as a symbol of Edward's sexual preferences and also to leave no external wounds. Following the insertion of a hollow cow horn, a red-hot poker was inserted into Edward's anus. In the west today homosexuality is being elevated to permit marriage but it remains against the law in many African and Muslim countries, sometimes punishable by death.

Two questions remain unanswered. The first is: why does homosexual love happen in man and virtually not at all the animal kingdom? The second is: what would happen if it became the norm?

In the animal kingdom, since Darwin we have come to accept that every species of living thing is under attack, either from other living things or from the environment. Some large animals eat smaller ones. Vegetarian animals compete for the available vegetation. The specimens that survive are those that, by instinct or by random chance, possess characteristics that suit them for survival. They breed, passing on genes to their young and training them in the survival techniques they learned from their parents. In the animal kingdom, the species that have survived are those in which the male is sexually drawn to the female when she is in season. Thus any female will automatically find a mate and will bring forth young to provide the next generation.

In humans the sense of smell has been greatly reduced over the millennia and now it is the appearance of the female that attracts the male, whether or not she is in season, fertile and capable of bearing children. Of course, it is not just the appearance that matters, but it is evident that pretty women attract men while plain ones as a rule do not. In other words, the attraction that makes for continuing human sexual relationships has much to do with appearance but little to do with procreation. This being so, it now becomes easier to understand why gay people can be attracted to each other. Procreation and fertility are not the issue, any more than between heterosexuals.

It remains true of course that the attraction between gay and straight couples is sexual, often highly so, but the sex act is quite distinct from bearing children. Some pregnancies are planned, many are not.

The discussion so far may seem far removed from the theory of time and energy. This is only partly so. Sexual man is the dimension which accounts for physical attraction. Spiritual man comes into the picture too. A marriage or live-in relationship based purely on physical attraction does not last long. Similarly, one which is purely a meeting of minds but without physical attraction is unlikely to succeed. The ideal relationship is one in which the sexual and spiritual dimensions are equal between the partners. In also helpful if both partners are the same distance along the economic axis.

As the relationship continues the partners' position on all three dimensions may change. Age may diminish the sexual dimension, though not always. The economic dimension may change with age. The spiritual dimension seems to be the one that changes least with age.

If the sexual dimension in a partnership gets out of balance, there is a risk that the more sexually driven partner —more commonly the man — will stray. Men find it easier than women to compartmentalise their sex lives. The man or woman may still care deeply for their partner and yet be able to compartmentalise this caring with the need for recreational sex with someone else.

Economic man in committed partnerships
The role of economic man in marriage or other committed partnerships has been understood in different societies and in different way. For example, the concept of the marriage dowry that was part of Victorian ethos and still prevails strongly in India is a reflection of a society where historically the wife kept the home and raised the children. The dowry represented capital that she brought with her to enable the husband to feed her and the children.

In the 19th and the first part of the 20th century it was still common in Europe for parents to make a settlement on their daughters when they married, but this is rare now. A trace of the concept remains in the tradition that the bride's parents pay for the wedding, but even this practice is no longer carved in stone. One in three couples in the UK who live together now are unmarried. Many who marry use the registry office and avoid the complexity and cost of a white wedding. Before children arrive both partners are likely to work and many mothers return to work a few months after the birth.

How does the theory of time and energy fit into the picture?

Courtship, cohabitation and divorce

Most couples live together before they marry or become an established item. This period may last for a few months to a year or two. The sexual dimension in man is the primary driver in courtship, coupled in some measure with the spiritual dimension. The couple discovers common interests, shared experiences and normally sleep together. They therefore have the opportunity to establish whether on these two dimensions they are roughly the same distance from the origin. If they are, the relationship is off to a good start; if not, it is flawed. For example, if the man wants sex every night and the woman resorts to headaches, or vice versa, tension ensues that is likely to doom the relationship. If the man enjoys serious television and the woman only mindless game-shows, or vice-versa, the ability to share common interests dwindles and the drift from each other begins.

In the early stages of courtship and cohabitation, the economic dimension is seemingly unimportant. If both partners are earning, the joint income is enough to ensure a satisfactory life-style. Indeed, the economies of sharing a roof and paying one rent or one mortgage instead of two increase the standard of living of both partners.

The arrival of the first child is the first major point at which the economic dimension of man enters the relationship, sometimes with a vengeance. The family income is reduced, perhaps halved, when the woman stops working. Babies entail initial costs that increase as they get older: clothes, food, hobbies, holidays and maybe private education. In fact all these, with the exception of private education, are minor costs in relation to the much larger one of the woman's income foregone. If the woman returns to work, a child-minder and possibly a cleaner reduce the net income she earns.

Reliance on the man's income brings further tension. The woman is dependent on that income. If it is paid into his account, he controls the cash. If it is paid into a joint account, there can be disputes over who has wasted money on what. Seldom is money paid direct into her account if she no longer works.

As we know, wages represent a claim on the time and energy of others, whether in the form of goods or of services. The man's earnings reflect the value placed on his time and energy by his employer. What he pays to the woman who stays at home, brings up his family, cooks his meals and cleans the house does not bear a direct relationship to the value of these services in the open market. Few are the couples who determine the amount of the house-keeping by calculating what the man would pay if he had a part-time cook, cleaner and full-time nanny instead of his partner. In addition, a full computation would need to include the going rate for a prostitute —

say £70 for half an hour —each time he had sex with her. As a result, because the woman's functions in the home are not costed, they are commonly undervalued.

It is a sad fact that the ecstasy of being in love is a fire that is too intense to last. The sexual dimension in both partners diminishes after the first few years. In some marriages sex becomes rare or non-existent after the first five to ten years. In a few cases sex happens hardly at all even in the first year. If the sexual dimension in both partners diminishes equally this need not matter. The problem is fundamental if the sexual urge diminishes in one partner more than the other. When this happens, it is all the more important that the other two dimensions, the spiritual and economic, remain balanced in the partnership.

The spiritual dimension, if it is in balance from the beginning, is the more robust of the two. If both partners share equally the feelings of love for their children, like the same sort of music, enjoy the same books and feel equally strongly about particular causes, these spiritual things may enable their relationship to survive even if the sexual dimension is out of balance. It is rare for partnerships to break up because one member suddenly becomes Buddhist, vegetarian, left-wing or addicted to bridge, but infidelity is one of the most common reasons for separation and divorce.

The importance of the economic dimension in a relationship cannot be underestimated. Both partners bring some economic assets to a relationship. One or both may have a property which is normally a person's largest single asset. They have savings and very likely both have an income. During the relationship they may accumulate a car, furniture, pictures and numerous household items that are paid for by one or the other from funds that in a real sense are jointly earned.

The economic dimension in man in the early stages of a relationship is largely suppressed, almost to the point of invisibility, by the sexual and spiritual dimensions. Perhaps the man always pays for dinner and the theatre when they are courting, or maybe they go Dutch. How little these things matter when they hold hands across a candlelit table. Perhaps one of them earns twice as much as the other; they don't care so long as they have each other. The electricity bill has to be paid; "can you do this one, darling?" "Of course, my sweet".

Then, as the sexual dimension of being passionately in love retreats to a more prosaic level, the economic dimension correspondingly resumes its normal role in each partner. At this point, even if they are comfortably off, the economic dimension can bring friction. If one earns much more than the other, he or she may feel entitled to spend more than the other. Either may make spending decisions of which the other disapproves. These frictions are magnified if the couple becomes short of money, particularly if one is out of work whether unemployed or through childbirth. Whose pen signs the cheques or settles the bills can be as potent a cause for friction as infidelity.

One in three marriages in the UK ends in divorce, and probably a similar or higher proportion of live-in relationships which are marriages in all but name, break up. When separation occurs, by definition the sexual relationship between the partners has fallen to zero. The spiritual dimension may still be there, for perhaps they still enjoy the same music and interests, but it has not proved enough to compensate for failure on the sexual dimension. As a result, the economic dimension becomes paramount. At the moment of separation, who owns what? There is an accumulation of jointly owned assets, there are savings in the bank and furnishings in the house all of which represent the couple's capitalised energy, and there remains a continuing stream of demands on their time and their current energy, of which the most important is the family. Someone must bring up the children and pay for their needs.

The anger and misery that accompany most separations and divorces are translated into the basic instincts and actions of economic man. The woman, if she is to bring up the children, feels primeval insecurity. She has often given up a career. The roof over her head may have to be sold. Life for her becomes a question of economic survival. In the man, if he is not to bring up the children, the new economic circumstances similarly awaken in him primeval instincts. His mate for whatever reason has failed him. Why should he be treated as a meal-ticket for life? It is common for women to demand from their husbands settlements representing half their joint earnings during the marriage. If the husband was earning a large income at the time and if the wife was a bimbo, a settlement on that basis can make a millionaire out of her for just a few years of bed-sharing. Economic woman realises that this is an opportunity too good to miss; economic man says he is being ripped off. Both hire lawyers and ultimately the courts impose a judgement.

In terms of time and energy the judgements imposed by the courts are frequently flawed because they assess the couple's assets at the time of divorcing without assessing separately the assets owned by each before the marriage. A simple and just way of calculating a financial settlement between couples who have no children is as follows.

The ratio of the net capital energy owned by each partner before the marriage should be the same at the time of divorce.

How does this work in practice? Here is a simplified example. The assets that the man and woman each brought to the partnership are listed and quantified at their then value. Suppose the ratio of capital energy on the wedding day was 3:1 in favour of the man. On the day of divorce they have their joint assets valued. These should be divided between them on a 3:1 ratio.

The attraction of such a system for allocating the capital value of the joint assets is that it is transparently fair. Further it eliminates all discussion of the myriad financial transactions that occurred during the marriage. If, for example, the man was the sole earner, that is immaterial. They both benefitted. If the man was mean and put most of his earnings into a private savings account, under this system his savings are included in the calculation of the joint net worth on the day of divorce, so the woman will take her share of it.

Marriage, or indeed any committed relationship between a couple living together reflects an attraction on all three dimensions: sexual, spiritual and economic. If all three dimensions are in balance between the two partners, even if the importance of the dimensions changes over time, the relationship will endure. The mistake that so many couples make is to marry quickly under the compelling drive of sexual man and to underestimate the significance of the economic and spiritual dimensions, both of which are longer lasting.

To the end of our life, economic man must be satisfied in all of us. Spiritual man may survive as an important part of the relationship. However, sexual man, who causes marriages to occur in the first place, lasts less than spiritual or economic man. Silvio Berlusconi, the turbulent Italian politician, continues unashamedly to pursue nubile women. Obviously his huge personal wealth makes the conquest of women much easier but the case of Berlusconi suggests that some men in their mid 70s are still well along the sexual dimension.

As for the other two dimensions, to the day we die we remain economic men. The shrivelled form in the hospice bed still enjoys a cup of tea and a hot meal to the very end and spiritual man may still enjoy a Mozart symphony from his bedside radio.

PART 3:
THE THEORY AS AN
EXPLANATION OF THE
FUTURE

30   WHY ECONOMIC MAN IS THE BEST PREDICTOR OF THE FUTURE

Can we test from observation whether economic man, spiritual man or sexual man are dependable predictors for the future?

Economic man has basic needs: food, clothing and shelter. Once these needs have been met, he does not starve or perish from exposure but he still wishes to increase the quantity or quality of the means to satisfy these basic needs. Staple food can be upgraded with more food of more variety cooked with more attention. Clothes cease to be a means of warmth but become a form of self-expression for the entertainment of self and others. A basic house consists of a roof and four walls within which economic man stays warm and dry. But this does not satisfy him. The house must be made larger, more beautiful, more convenient. It becomes an extension of his individuality and a storehouse for his possessions.

Even if economic man is satisfied with his food, drink, house and clothing, his desires remain unfulfilled. He accumulates further possessions. When he has an abundance of these, there remain services of many kinds which he wishes to obtain: gardeners, accountants, car repairers, holidays, concerts, theatre visits, opera; the list is endless.

The living proof that economic man goes on being acquisitive is seen in some multi-millionaires. They continue to work, to do deals, to buy and sell companies, develop property and play the stock exchange long after they have any idea of how many millions they are worth. From all this it seems clear that economic man is predictable in his motivation and hence his actions.

What of spiritual man? He is far less predictable. Some examples from history support this statement. St Paul's conversion on the road to Damascus remains a byword for change of outlook and motive. Today numerous religious orders, cults and organisations succeed in changing the beliefs, outlook and behaviour of spiritual man. Some Christian denominations are "born again". Organisations such as Scientologists, Moonies and a variety of group therapy systems aim to change spiritual man, and they can do so. In Muslim countries the unpredictability of religious devotees is regularly seen. In Iraq and other parts of the Middle East Shi'ites launch suicide attacks on Sunnis and vice-versa.

There remain sexual man and woman. How predictable are they? The answer is not very. In most western societies social behaviour is relatively free from constraint. People marry and divorce, live together and split up and have relationships sequentially or simultaneously. The partners may be of the opposite or same gender. Marriage between people of the same gender has just been recognized in the UK and several European nations. Formal polygamy was permitted briefly by the Mormons of the USA but is not permitted in the west. Some Muslim men have four principal wives together with "minor wives" or mistresses. The number of wives is seen as an indication of affluence and manhood. The rules about marriage and other relationships have varied through time, suggesting that sexual man is an unpredictable creature. In the animal kingdom swans are a rare species that mate for life. Man sometimes does so but as a rule he does not.

Of the three characteristics that make up each of us — economic, spiritual and sexual — the former dominates in most people most of the time and therefore is the more predictable in relations to the present and the future.

Ian Senior: *Time and Energy*

31   THE WEALTH OF NATIONS

Nations' wealth lies in attributes that can be grouped under two headings: physical wealth and intellectual wealth.

Physical wealth comprises
- geography and climate
- fertile land
- access to sea
- fossil fuel reserves
- mineral reserves

Intellectual wealth comprises:
- intelligence
- education
- creativity
- motivation

We shall now consider in turn the impact of each of these in creating material wealth.

Geography and climate

Until the advent of man, the world's climate depended entirely on the sun and still largely does so. Scientists who study weather, quaintly still known as meteorologists, have studied changes in the world's climate that have taken place over millennia. Some changes have been major such as the various ice-ages that lasted for thousands of years. Others in the timescale of planet Earth have been minor, for example mild or severe winters. The role of man up to the 19th century was localised and insignificant. He cut down some forests and altered the landscape by farming but he worked with the climate and responded to it.

In the 19th century, the harnessing of fossil fuel for energy produced the first significant man-made pollution. Factories belched smoke into the air and discharged untreated waste into rivers, lakes and the sea. The effects were unpleasant but mainly localised. However, the harnessing of cheap fossil energy coupled with discovery of electricity and the internal combustion engine meant that man's ability to alter the environment began to grow rapidly. A self-reinforcing cycle began. The better man became at finding and harnessing fossil energy, the more of it he required and the easier it was to obtain. The energy needed to drill for more energy was minor in relation to the supplies of energy obtained through drilling.

In the same way, man's ability to alter the landscape progressed by orders of magnitude. To fell a tree before the invention of the chain-saw required considerable human time and energy with an axe or saw. Today a few men with chain-saws and logging equipment can clear forests in days.

The demands of economic man, the consumer, are insatiable for food and consumer goods of all kinds. The application of chemicals to farming produced major short-term gains in the quantity of food. Factories and power stations have all continued to expand output to satisfy the demands of a world population growing in numbers and, at least in the west, in length of life.

It can be seen, therefore, that at the heart of continuing

industrialisation and its impact on the planet's environment, is energy. As noted at the start of this book, all energy, however it is used or transformed, ends up as heat. In its most direct route, fossil fuel such as coal is burned in the grate once and the heat escapes to the atmosphere. Food is consumed and turned into kilocalories which are given off mainly as body-heat. Petrol is burned in a car's engine and much of its energy is lost to atmosphere as heat. The remainder powers the car's motion.

Three facts have emerged in the past decade on which there is now universal agreement. The first is that individual companies, conurbations and countries can damage the environment easily but to preserve it requires thought, democracy and national self-denial. The second is that their actions may have impact on countries close by or thousands of miles away. The third is that the cumulative impact of all industrial actions has begun to disturb the balance of the world's environment. Climate change, global warming, the "green-house effect" and the destruction of the ozone layer are widely recognized though scientists may disagree about the timing and severity of the impact to be expected over the next 100 years. The amount of carbon that is expelled to atmosphere is now generally seen as a significant factor in climate change.

Most nations are now awakening to the realisation that their geography is an asset that must be preserved even if immediate economic pressures make this difficult. In South America rain forests are still being cleared at a frightening rate to provide timber exports and land for growing bio-fuels. Some forests in Canada and the USA are brown from acid rain. The Great Lakes of North America are dead from pollution. The natural wealth of the environment as a source of life is being squandered by the activities of economic man.

Earlier, I attributed warfare to economic man. Far worse ravages of the planet may yet occur. Chemical weapons are cheaper to produce, though less easy to control, than traditional or nuclear bombs. Following the defeat and expulsion of Iraq from Kuwait in 1991 Iraqi arsenals of chemical and biological weapons were destroyed by the United Nations. The danger from Iraq may temporarily be past but Syria has stocks of chemical and biological weapons and on 21 August 2013, the Syrian government used them against civilians with 1,300 killed in the attack including 300 children.

Nuclear weapons, unused since Hiroshima and Nagasaki, have multiplied in number, sophistication, destructive power and range. The bombs that destroyed the two Japanese cities are insignificant in destructive power compared with the multiple warheads carried today by a single nuclear submarine or other delivery systems.

Despite the fact that for half a century since the end of the second world war nuclear weapons have been available but not used is a tribute to a balance of power that meant that the owners of the weapons, primarily the USA and Russia, knew that however effective a first strike might be, nothing would avoid second strike retaliation with mutually assured destruction (aptly known as MAD) on a horrendous scale. The challenge today is to persuade the unstable regimes of India, Pakistan, the middle-east, Iran and North Korea that MAD is a reality.

If we take an optimistic view that in the next decade democracy, good sense and humanity will replace religious fanaticism and political tyranny in the aforementioned countries, there still remains the problem of preserving the world's geography and climate.

Economic man operates out of self-interest. If his factory belches toxins into the air, it is because it is in his economic interest to do so. The task of governments and individuals now is to make economic man aware that it is in his self-interest to preserve the environment. Progress in this direction is encouraging. The role of government used to be seen as preventing pollution. Now it is becoming seen as making polluters pay for their deeds.

The increasing awareness of green issues provides a tool for consumers to curb the polluting tendencies of economic man. Governments' role must be to ban environmentally harmful substances and to make consumers aware of harmless alternatives. The case of lead-free petrol is an example of how governments can penalise the users of the harmful product (leaded petrol) by making them pay higher duty — effectively a tax on polluters.

The use of taxes benignly to safeguard the environment should be seen as an accepted role of government in aligning the self-interest of economic man with the needs of the environment and indeed of spiritual man. The case for taxes on smoking and alcohol are analogous. Smokers and drinkers pollute mainly their own bodies but in doing so they impose costs on society and the health services that have to care for diseases caused by tobacco and alcohol. Estimates have been made of the cost to public funds of treating tobacco and alcohol related diseases. However, the case is not clear cut. Some researchers say that the duty received by the British government of about £9.5bn a year in tax adequately pays for NHS costs of treating people with diseases caused by tobacco and alcohol.

It is increasingly clear that the wealth of an individual nation deriving from its climate can be harmed by the behaviour of economic men and nations in other parts of the globe.

Fertile land

Arable land produces food directly. Grazing land supports animals which in turn provide food as meat or dairy products. The quality of the land for producing food depends to a large extent on the climate and geological factors. The best soil is generally used to grow grain and the worst remains as grazing. Soil of intermediate quality may be used for growing vegetables or fruit.

For hundreds of years economic man has experimented with ways of obtaining higher yields from a given piece of land. In the Middle Ages he found that if he rotated the crops under the three field system, he could increase yields at no additional expenditure of time or energy. The use of animal and human dung is mentioned in Chaucer. It was indeed a bonus for economic man to discover that a relatively small expenditure of time and energy in spreading a waste product gave a worth-while increase in yield. Modern farmers found that by applying artificial fertilisers and pesticides, they could increase the yield by considerably more than the cost to them in terms of time, energy or money.

Today, there is evidence that high yields cannot be sustained indefinitely by these methods. Further, consumer resistance is mounting against foodstuffs grown in this way. Genetically modified crops are claimed to increase yields but there is considerable consumer resistance against them. Health-food shops, organic food and vegetarian eating used to be seen as fringe operations for fringe people. Today every restaurant offers vegetarian dishes in its menus. Periodic scares about meat, for example mad cow disease, also help to move opinion towards organic food, generally of a vegetarian nature.

An interesting phenomenon is that the move towards healthy eating appears to be motivated by both economic and spiritual man. Economic man has woken up to the barrage of medical evidence that a healthy diet reduces the risk of heart attacks, bowel cancer and other major illnesses. He enjoys his food and drink but he can also see the value of not dying prematurely or having major surgery. He finds it difficult to adjust to a simpler diet and to cut down the calories that taste so delightful. When he does so, it is purely from self-interest.

Spiritual man also enjoys food and drink, but when he becomes aware of the methods which are used to produce some forms of factory food he finds them repellent. At a level of pure humanity, he cannot accept the conditions of battery hens, the treatment of calves to produce white veal and the practice of adding the refuse of the slaughter-houses back into the feed of animals that later will be driven into the slaughter-houses. Spiritual man is making a stand against these practices and he is aligned with economic man's wish to avoid eating contaminated food.

A further consideration will steadily increase influence on both spiritual man and economic man: eating animals is a highly inefficient use of land as the primary source of food. The wastefulness of meat is measurable. One hundred tonnes of grain, legumes and soya fed to cattle produces 18 tonnes of meat. Thus the pleasure of eating meat is highly wasteful of original food. Further, to the space required for growing cattle feed must be added the space needed for grazing the cattle. Production of meat is an extravagance that future generations may find unacceptable.

Further considerations influence spiritual man. The first is that in some countries, because of government intervention into the market for agricultural commodities, there are substantial surpluses while in other parts of the world, notably Africa, there is widespread malnutrition and starvation. The food surpluses of the USA and the European Union gave rise to the policies of "set aside" which give farmers payments for *not* producing crops that turned into "mountains" or "lakes" in the case of wine. Such surpluses simply showed that market forces have not been allowed to work. But they also show that surpluses can be produced which in turn can and should be channelled to the starving areas of Africa providing that ways can be found not to put local growers out of business.

Economic man remains unconcerned about starvation in Africa. He points out that much of the tragedy is self-inflicted and derives from civil wars, corrupt governments and the absence of democracy. The alternative forms of government, whether full-blooded socialism in Ethiopia, war-lords in Somalia or residual tribalism in most other African states, have eliminated or undermined democracy leaving only the primitive instincts of lawless economic man to grab from others what they have produced rather than produce anything at all.

Economic man is aware that if the industrialised northern hemisphere does nothing, the problems of Africa in particular will go away in the Malthusian sense via disease and starvation. Spiritual man, however, sends contributions to Oxfam in the hope that these will be used to alleviate starvation today and to create the means of production for tomorrow. At gatherings of wealthy nations commitments are made to give 0.7 per cent of national product to bettering the situation in Africa and other impoverished nation states. The promises made by politicians on these occasions often are not honoured.

As fossil fuels begin to run out, the availability of agricultural land will resume importance in the wealth of each nation. Artificial fertilizers are all dependent on energy. Phosphates, for example, require considerable energy to mine, transport and lay on the land.

The green movement, still young in political terms, has been set in motion by spiritual man, and economic man is beginning to join in for reasons of self-interest. Green principles have already been widely accepted because they appeal to spiritual man and economic man alike. Farmers must stop leeching the soil with phosphates because the cost of doing to will rise and the destructive effects of doing so will be universally apparent. Less needs to be grown on a given area of land but in an environmentally friendly way.

This conclusion is worrying for the starving of Africa. When there are no food surpluses in the industrialized world, economic men who will always to be in the majority will send no further aid and will trade only the food which African and other states can afford to pay for in hard currency. Oxfam and the other relief agencies will still be at work but the surpluses will have gone. As the golden age of cheap energy wanes, so also will the golden age of abundant cheap food. Africa has to turn away from the inefficiency of corrupt tribalism and civil war and instead concentrate on learning to farm the land to the point of self-sufficiency.

Robert Mugabe, Zimbabwe's first president who is still in office after 33 years and at least one blatantly rigged election, exemplifies all that is worst about political systems in Africa. He ruined Zimbabwe's once successful farming industry by expropriating the country's white owned farms giving them to cronies. In true African style, he is building himself a mansion out of public funds and has won another five years as president in an election where malpractice was widespread.

Access to the sea
Three quarters of the earth's surface is covered by water or ice. As a basis for the production of vegetation and fish the sea is akin to soil. It produces relatively small quantities of vegetable matter compared with soil but, like soil, it supports a vast range of animal life. It provides a habitat for a small group of mammals such as whales and dolphins that need air to breathe but cannot live on dry land, and for a variety of birds such as penguins and animals such as seals that are at home on land or in the water and need both for survival.

The value of the sea to economic man has increased dramatically in the past 50 years. Fishing methods have become increasingly sophisticated. Large nets pulled by powerful ships produce huge catches that deplete the fish stocks. Whaling is now rejected by most environmentally conscious nations. The exceptions are Norway which kills whales for their meat and Japan which does so too under the hypocritical justification of "scientific research". Timely action by the International Whaling Commission has succeeded in stabilising the remaining population of whales, some species of which were threatened with extinction.

Economic man has frequently polluted the sea by releasing into it untreated sewage and radio-active waste intentionally and crude oil and toxic chemicals unintentionally. The result is that the future value of the sea as a source of abundant food is in jeopardy. High levels of toxic waste have been found in wild and in farmed fish making them dangerous to eat.

The gravity of the problem has been known for years to environmentalists and is now beginning to become part of the wider green consciousness. The timing of awareness of marine pollution coincides with a trend away from eating red meat and towards seafood. Some countries, notably Japan, have always eaten fish as part of the staple diet. Medical evidence supports the view that a fish-based diet is healthier than one based on red meat which contains a far higher proportion of fat.

In the west, the attraction of food from the sea will accelerate because of health considerations. Periodical alarms such as the emergence of mad cow disease temporarily reduce demand for meat. The future value of fishing rights will increase the more that demand for farmed red meat declines.

Will economic man make efforts to preserve the sea from further pollution and prevent it from being fished dry? The signs are positive. One of the benefits of being comfortably fed is that economic man can plan for the future. A starving man eats the seed corn of next year's harvest. A well fed man has time to think how next year's harvest can feed him and his family even better.

In the past the difficulty of conserving the sea lay in how to enforce preservation policies. It was almost impossible to know who was catching too much fish, who was dumping untreated waste into the sea and which tankers were leaking oil or pumping out contaminated bilge. The incredible advance of science is rapidly solving many of these questions. Effluents can be monitored and this is already happening. Supra-national bodies such as the European Commission list beaches whose water fails purity standards. Satellites that were developed for military purposes can monitor shipping's activities in fine detail and oil slicks can be traced to the ships that produce them. Scientists can now make a digital "finger print" of oil according to its chemistry. Thus if every oil tanker leaves a specimen of its cargo before sailing, a sample of any oil slick could be traced to the tanker and a fine imposed.

From the view-point of both justice and economics these developments are admirable. In the past, the cost of dealing with pollution was borne by tax-payers in general. In future, individual polluters will be made to pay for their actions in the same way that on-the-spot fines are imposed in Singapore for those who drop litter.

Mineral reserves
Minerals are indispensable for making things. Before the discovery of iron and the invention of steel, man had only wood, stone, bone and other products derived from animals as the basic materials for artefacts. All these had value as functional items. Gold and silver

were discovered later and, being soft, came to be valued for their appearance rather than for functionality, a role they still have today as jewellery.

Making bronze and, later, iron and steel had the effect not only of making these minerals valuable but of adding value to many others. For example, the production of steel required coke for the furnaces and coal acquired value as an input to making steel. The more steel was made and harnessed with steam power, the more metal tools, machines, vehicles, ships and buildings could be made. This in turn stimulated demand for steel and the sophisticated chemicals needed to make better, specialised steel. Thus, by a circular process, energy stimulated the value of minerals and these stimulated demand for energy.

The value attached to minerals completely reversed the relative wealth of some tracts of land. The value of rich farm-land increases many times if minerals such as bauxite for aluminium, phosphates, iron ore, copper or rare earths are discovered. Countries with mineral deposits such as Australia and South Africa achieved new found wealth in the nineteenth and twentieth centuries.

The value of all metals and other minerals is determined by supply and demand on world markets. They are traded in specialist commodity exchanges. Their prices fluctuate on a day to day basis, sometimes by the hour, according to the needs of manufacturers who require them as inputs to their products. Their value, as indicated in their market price, can change in the long term as in the short. For example, copper which once was the main conductor in telecommunication equipment, has seen glass fibres replace it in cables. Tin, once a basic material in the food canning business, has seen aluminium and steel supplant it in many applications.

The conclusion is clear. Minerals represent an important asset in the wealth of nations but the value of the assets fluctuates. Further, to extract, process and fabricate the minerals requires large quantities of natural energy. Thus the value of minerals in the wealth of nations is a reflected value of the existence of energy.

Fossil fuel reserves

As is the recurring theme of this book, fossil fuel reserves are at present the fundamental though finite source of most natural energy. Hence they are the origin of most production and of most wealth in the world today. Though other forms of the wealth of nations also represent assets, all of them require energy for realising the potential value of the asset. Minerals need energy to extract, transport, process and fabricate them. Agricultural land needs tractors. Sea-going ships require energy because wind-power is unpredictable.

Take away energy, and the value of most other national assets falls. With only his own energy and that of animals, man would be almost unable to exploit the other forms of national wealth and would revert to tilling the land by hand, horse and ox.

Four forms of intellectual wealth

All forms of the wealth of nations discussed so far have concerned tangible, measurable objects such as climate, water, minerals, gold and fossil fuels. Yet there are four forms of *intellectual* wealth that must also be considered:

- natural intelligence;
- education;
- creativity; and
- motivation.

These four exist in different proportions in every individual and hence collectively in every group of individuals, race or nation. Like all aspects of the mind they can be recognised and measured to some extent, though not with the accuracy that physical objects can be measured. They can be thought of as four separate characteristics that make up an individual's or a nation's intellectual wealth.

Natural intelligence
Some individuals have more natural intelligence than others, just as some can run faster than others. Whether this intelligence comes from heredity or up-bringing (sometimes called 'nature versus nurture') has been debated endlessly. What is clear is that by the time individuals reach adulthood there are major differences between them. IQ and aptitude tests are ways of measuring these differences. An individual with below average IQ may do a worth-while job as a labourer or porter but he could not attempt to be a lecturer in nuclear physics. The lecturer in nuclear physics, however, might prefer not to be a labourer but he stands a reasonable prospect of holding down the job.

If there are clear and measurable differences in the natural intelligence of individuals within a nation, are there differences in natural intelligence between nations or ethnic groups? This is a delicate subject and conclusions that suggest there *are* differences in national IQs between groups arouse fierce hostility. While anybody can notice the heavy predominance of black athletes in the Olympic finals of the 100m and other sprint events, it is considered racist to suggest there may be other differences between ethnic groups.

The Bell Curve by Herrnstein and Murray (1996) considers this subject in meticulous detail. The authors conclude that there are differences in the collective IQs of certain ethnic groups. Their book provides copious data, some of it based on admissions to 26 top US universities analysed by four ethnic groups: black, Asian, Latino and white. In 17 out of 26 universities Asians gained scholastic aptitude test results (SATs) significantly above the mean for whites. In all 26 universities blacks' results were significantly below white and Asian. Latinos' scores lay between white and black. These are among the findings of an 800 page, copiously referenced book[11].

Do these findings matter? Only if a high IQ or SAT score are the only criteria that matter in life. Economic man may benefit from having a higher IQ than others but for spiritual man or for sexual man there is no obvious need for a high IQ. If utility or happiness is the real goal of life it is first necessary to have food, shelter and warmth. After that, it is not obvious that university teachers are happier and more contented than people with lower IQs who may in some circumstances be earning much more. Many professional sportsmen, notably footballers, earn as much in a week (£30,000 upwards) as many people earn in a year. If earnings relate to happiness or utility, top athletes come out on top whatever their IQ.

Casual observation suggests that there are more black footballers in

---

11   Herrnstein R J and Murray C 1996. Free Press Paperbacks, p452

top European clubs than their ethnic percentages in the countries to which the clubs belong. Clearly some have been recruited from Africa where the wages for top players are much lower than in Europe. Even so, there seems to be a provisional case that black athletes are better than white, at least when it comes to the world's most universal game, association football.

It seems reasonable to conclude that there may be differences in natural ethnically-based intelligence or scholastic aptitude just as there may be differences in ethnically-based sporting ability.

If utility could be measured precisely by income, economic man would undoubtedly prefer to have a high IQ. It does seem as though the main troubles faced by the world — wars, climate change, potential food shortages, misgovernment and corruption —result from the activities of economic man. The teachings of spiritual man have too often been ignored or have been hijacked by economic men for their own selfish purposes.

Education

All sentient creatures learn by experience which typically is a combination of pleasure and pain. Darwin's theory of the survival of the fittest, when linked with memory, enables sentient creatures to remember the result of previous actions. They repeat the actions if the outcome was pleasurable but avoid them if it was painful. Innumerable experiments with animals have found that they can learn through reward and punishment.

Education at a human level consists of passing on inherited knowledge so that each generation is spared having to reinvent the wheel. Education can be thought of as a technology for transferring knowledge. The more efficient the transfer process, the more quickly the students reach the point where they have sufficient knowledge or skills to become productive members of society.

An educational system is part of a nation's wealth. Within the western world league tables are established showing attainment in basic skills between countries. It is also apparent that educational systems are better funded and more effective in the industrialised world than those in the third world where illiteracy is still prevalent

Creativity
Invention and discovery both constitute creativity. An inventor is clearly creative. A discoverer can also be described as creative since an enquiring mind must be the precursor to discovering anything. Some important discoveries such as penicillin occur by chance but these are likely to be the exception rather than the rule. Economic progress results from invention and discovery. The person who invented the wheel ushered in a new era of civilisation. Steam power enabled railways to be built and factories to mass-produce. The discovery of penicillin and antibiotics has saved innumerable lives.

Creativity is hard to define but easy to recognise. Some creativity takes the form of painstaking research inevitably coupled with trial and error. At other times creativity may be a blinding flash of inspiration as when Archimedes, in his bath, realised how the volume of any object could be measured by its displacement of water. Or again, invention may happen by mistake. It seems likely that the fermentation of grape-juice into wine happened unintentionally to begin with.

From observation it seems that some people are born with creativity while others are not. Similarly, some are born good athletes while others' bodies or reflexes have the wrong characteristics to become good athletes however hard they try. Research suggests that people whose brains are dominated by the right half are left-handed and are more prone to be creative. The majority of us in whom left sided brains dominate are right handed and possibly more practical than creative.

Can any nation be judged above or below average in creativity? Seven firms whose inventions have revolutionised modern living in the last 40 years — IBM, Microsoft, Apple, Facebook, Amazon, E-Bay and Twitter — are all from the USA.

Motivation
Any teacher or employer knows the importance of motivation in students and employees. Where does motivation come from? There is no easy answer. Some argue that parental influence and the culture of the society in which a child is reared are decisive. Others believe that motivation is inherited with genes. Most of us can think of counter-examples, namely children from professional homes who have dropped out of society and conversely of children from disadvantaged homes who have worked their way to the top with no help from their parents.

Are some nations or ethnic groups more motivated in economic matters than others? From observation, it seems that they are. It also seems possible to put forward some plausible explanations. For example, economic motivation demonstrably flourishes in market economies compared with in those controlled by the state. West

Germany was far more prosperous than East Germany before reunification. Before unification South Vietnam was far more prosperous than North Vietnam. South Korea is thriving and prosperous compared with North Korea where millions have starved to death.

In much of the former Soviet Union despite having plentiful natural resources, bread queues, shortages and lack of choice were the norm. In essence, demand exceeded supply. By contrast in the west every shop is stocked with goods because supply exceeds demand. Clearly, economic systems which reward individuals provide economic motivation while those that depend on a collective ideal such as socialism are less successful, frequently disastrously so.

A second possible explanation of motivation is the need to survive in an alien country or culture. It seems possible that people who emigrate have more motivation in the first place which causes them to migrate. Unquestionably if they are to succeed they have to work harder than locals in the new country. The overseas Chinese in Singapore, Malaysia and the south-east Asian region are renowned for their hard work. In England, immigrant south Asians have carved a niche by running small groceries which stay open for long hours, and people of Indian and Pakistani origin have become successful in several professions, notably healthcare, accountancy and law.

The dynamic of the USA is sometimes attributed to the fact that it is a nation of immigrants. The state of Israel, founded in 1948, also supports the survivalist theory of economic motivation. Since its formation it has been under permanent threat of attack from neighbouring Arab states and for some years under intermittent rocket fire from Gaza. The economic motivation of Israel as a nation state is observable.

A third theory about national or ethnic motivation relates to climate. It is suggested that where the climate is warm and the soil is fertile, economic man survives with little expenditure of personal energy. Economic man in the cold north, however, has to make houses and to harvest enough food in summer to see him through the winter. National economic motivation, according to this theory, is more often found in nations in cold parts of the world. The theory is supported by the wealth of the northern nations of Europe, the USA and Japan compared with the poverty of much of South America, south Asia and most of Africa.

Nobel prizes

It seems clear that the four aspects of a nation's intellectual wealth can be recognised but cannot easily be measured. One comparison can be used to test the theory that different nations and ethnic groups have different levels and pools of intellectual wealth. The Nobel Foundation in Sweden awards prizes for achievement in physics, chemistry, medicine and economics. The first three categories are those which are clearly dependent on man's intellect. It is less certain that economics, a discipline with moveable goalposts, qualifies as a science.

As shown in the table below, in 2000-2012, the USA won 42 Nobel prizes for physics, chemistry and medicine; the UK and Japan each won 10, France and Germany won 4, Russia won 3, China won 2, India and Canada each one 1. Brazil, one of the world's rapidly industrialising countries did not win any. The final column adjusts for population with a ratio of the number of Nobel prizes divided by the population (times 1,000). It suggests that nations' intellectual wealth, as measured in this simple way, is much higher in some industrialised countries than others. How long these differences will last in the face of competition from India, China and Brazil remains to be seen.

Nobel Prizes in Chemistry, Physics and Medicine,
Selected countries 2000-2012

Country	Prizes	Pop M	Ratio
USA	42	316	133.1
UK	10	63	158.2
Japan	10	127	78.5
France	4	66	61.0
Germany	4	82	48.8
Russia	3	143	20.9
China	2	1,345	1.5
Canada	1	35	28.5
India	1	1,210	0.8
Brazil	0	194	-

To say that the table measures nations' general IQ or scholastic aptitude would be misleading since a Nobel prize represents the pinnacle of a nation's intellectual achievers and gives no information about the level of education and intellect below the pinnacle. Nevertheless we can assume that various conditions are needed to produce Nobel Prize winners: good intellect, education, research facilities and motivation.

From the analysis of this chapter I conclude that not only are there significant differences in the material wealth of nations, which is self-evident, but that there are likely to be significant differences between the intellectual wealth of nations and ethnic groups. If this is so, it has important implications for the future. A nation that possesses few natural resources, notably fossil energy, must live with this disadvantage. However, if it has intellectual wealth, including motivation, we can expect it to redress the balance.

32   MEASURING THE WEALTH OF NATIONS

Most people, though not all, want to be wealthy. Wealth in simplest terms means food, warmth, comfort and security. At a more sophisticated level, wealth means possessions, access to services and power over people. The minority who intentionally renounce wealth are likely to be people who score highly on the spiritual dimension, typically monks, nuns and others with religious callings. Tramps and drop-outs who sleep rough may not have consciously renounced wealth and may have done so unwillingly through bad luck, bad health or addiction to alcohol and drugs.

Wealth, of course, is relative. A typical home in western Europe, with a refrigerator, deep-freeze, television set, washing-machine, hi-fi audio equipment, telephone and a car would be considered luxurious in developing countries. Since economic man wants to be wealthy, he measures and compares wealth. People when thinking of changing jobs scan the newspapers to find out if they are being paid enough in their present position. Unions, when they negotiate for their members, compare their wages with those of other unions.

At national level, tables are published listing the 100 or so wealthiest people in a given country. In general wealthy people are admired particularly if their wealth is self-made. In the USA to be wealthy is the ultimate social accolade and it is considered normal to ask and tell other people how much you earn. This is taboo in the UK.

Making comparisons of wealth between nations is relatively easy. All nations publish national accounts which state the country's gross domestic product. This is a measure of what the country has produced in a year. The figure is converted into US$ at the prevailing exchange rate, and divided by the number of citizens to provide GDP per head, expressed in US$. This simple concept enables the wealth of countries to be compared. Sometimes a further adjustment is made, namely apply purchasing power parity to the figures of GDP per head in US$. This is an attempt to provide a better comparison in terms of the standard of living between nations.

How useful is GDP per head? As a measure of *current wealth* it is fine, but it does not tell us anything about a nation's *capital wealth*. Reserves of natural energy in the form of oil, gas and coal are shown below.

Because all wealth derives from natural energy, I suggest that to measure the wealth of nations it is necessary to compare both what they earn now, namely their current flow of revenue; and also what they have in reserve for the future, their capital wealth. GDP per capita is a commonly used measure of a country's current wealth. As noted above, figures have been adjusted by purchasing power parity (PPP). A given basket of goods costs more to buy in international $ terms in different countries and PPP adjusts for this.

Current wealth of nations
It will be seen from the following table that some oil and gas rich nations come high up the table of currently wealthy nations, notably Qatar, Norway, Brunei, UAE and Kuwait. Luxembourg has built its wealth on a successful banking community. Singapore also has no mineral or fossil fuel resources but has built its economy on free trade allied with financial services.

Selected countries, GDP (PPP) per capita, 2010-11

International $

Qatar	98,498
Luxembourg	80,559
Singapore	59,710
Norway	53,396
Brunei	49,536
Hong Kong	49,417
USA	48,328
UAE	47,729
Switzerland	44,452
San Marino	43,090
Netherlands	42,023
Kuwait	41,701
Austria	41,556
Australia	40,847
Ireland	40,838
Sweden	40,705
Canada	40,519
Germany	38,077
Iceland	38,060
Belgium	37,781
Taiwan	37,716
Denmark	37,048
UK	36,552
Finland	35,981
France	35,068
Japan	34,748
European Union	31,673

Source: IMF on Wikipedia

Capital wealth

As discussed in part 1 of this book, energy is either stored as capital wealth or consumed as current wealth. Interestingly, the word 'current' means 'at the present time' and also power as in 'electric current'. Since without energy most other resources are useless, the ultimate source of a nation's capital wealth is its stored energy. This concept cuts across traditional economic thinking. As noted in chapter 18 central banks store 'wealth' in the form of gold or convertible currencies, notably US$. These currencies have no value as such. They are not even bank-notes when they are stored in central banks. They are just figures on paper or in computers that represent the accumulated claims on resources that one country may make on another.

The position of gold was also discussed in chapter 17. As a metal its practical use, apart from jewellery, plating for electronic components and capping teeth, is nil but its limited supply and intrinsic beauty have made it a store of value which has become accepted world-wide.

In theory then, it might seem logical to measure the *capital wealth* of nations by measuring the value of gold and hard currencies in $ per head in each of their central banks. The reason for not doing so is that these reserves can fluctuate quite sharply. Further, the value of gold itself, measured in US$ or any other hard currency, can also move significantly on world exchanges.

Since energy is the real source of all wealth, it seems more logical to measure nations' energy reserves per head rather than their gold or currency reserves. This system for measuring wealth produces dramatically different results for some countries.

The following table shows the extraction of oil and gas by 17 of the world's most endowed countries, their reserves and the number of years remaining if they continue to extract at the same rate. The conclusion is that at present extraction rates, and without the discovery of important new fields, there are enough reserves to last for 64 years. This can be thought of as the period of remission during which the world must learn to develop renewable or possibly atomic energy. The reserves themselves and the rate of extraction vary widely between countries.

The time horizon is roughly three generations. Children being born today will have to live in a very different world by the time they retire.

Summary of oil and gas reserves, 2012

Country	Reserves 10^9 bbl	Reserves 10^9 m³	Production 10^6 bbl/d	Production 10^3 m³/d	Reserve life [1] years
Venezuela	296.5	47.14	2.1	330	387
Saudi Arabia	265.4	42.20	8.9	1,410	81
Canada	175	27.8	2.7	430	178
Iran	151.2	24.04	4.1	650	101
Iraq	143.1	22.75	2.4	380	163
Kuwait	101.5	16.14	2.3	370	121
United Arab Emirates	136.7	21.73	2.4	380	156
Russia	74.2	11.80	9.7	1,540	21

Summary of oil and gas reserves, 2012

Country	Reserves 10^9 bbl	Reserves 10^9 m^3	Production 10^6 bbl/d	Production 10^3 m^3/d	Reserve life [1] years
Kazakhstan	49	7.8	1.5	240	55
Libya	47	7.5	1.7	270	76
Nigeria	37	5.9	2.5	400	41
Qatar	25.41	4.040	1.1	170	63
China	20.35	3.235	4.1	650	14
United States	26.8	4.26	7.0	1,110	10
Angola	13.5	2.15	1.9	300	19
Algeria	13.42	2.134	1.7	270	22
Brazil	13.2	2.10	2.1	330	17
Total of top seventeen reserves	1,324	210.5	56.7	9,010	64

Notes:

1 <u>Reserve to Production ratio</u> (in years), calculated as reserves / annual production. (from above)

Source. http://en.wikipedia.org/wiki/Oil_reserves

33   WHEN FOSSIL FUELS RUN SHORT

Before the days of ubiquitous credit cards, some of us can recall holidays when we took a specified amount in foreign cash and travellers' cheques and knew we had to make the money last for the full holiday. We may have experienced spending rather lavishly in the first week only to find ourselves counting our notes and coins on the last days and wondering how to keep enough for a bottle of duty-free at the airport. Nations are composed of people who finally are beginning to count up the notes and coins which represent reserves of energy. Oil and gas are in finite supply in the world. More reserves will be discovered but the most accessible oil and gas fields have already been found.

Clearly oil and gas reserves will not simply stop on a single day like a tap being turned off. Those countries whose reserves are tapering off, as in the UK, will use them more carefully. The price of oil and gas measured in US$ has already begun to rise noticeably. This will make people more economical in consuming natural energy and in doing so their standard of living will fall. Cars will become smaller and people will use them less. Air flights for overseas holidays will become more expensive which in turn will reduce the market for holidays abroad. Business meetings will increasingly take place by video links.

Although the world still has considerable reserves of coal, a return to coal as a major supplier of natural energy seems unlikely so long as oil, gas and nuclear power are available. Coal is much less easy to extract than oil and gas. When near the surface its extraction scars the landscape. Underground, it is difficult to extract and bring to the surface. Coal burning power stations give off more carbon than oil and gas. Despite modern advances, mining remains a dirty and dangerous activity. For this reason, economic man prefers to exploit oil and gas which conveniently push their way to the surface when the drill reaches them and are much easier to transport and process than coal.

Accessing natural gas between layers of the ground, known as "fracking", has aroused much interest as well as scepticism. What is certain is that even if the technology can be mastered and proved safe, the cost per unit of gas obtained will be considerably more expensive than for gas from the fields that have been exploited up to now. The actual amount of gas obtainable this way may only be a tenth of the volume that available from existing traditional wells.

To many, nuclear fuel seems an obvious solution to take over from oil and gas when these run short. Despite the Chernobyl and Fukushima disasters, a number of countries consider that nuclear power should be developed as the main supply of energy to keep the lights on. Wind and water power alone are unlikely to be reliable enough or to provide the amount of electricity needed to replace oil and gas.

The future of world energy production and consumption can now be forecast with some confidence. Oil and gas production which increased up to the turn of century will decline. If new fields are found, for example in the south Atlantic, present levels of production may continue for a decade or two. The countries with major reserves such as Saudi Arabia and Venezuela may increase production but still raise prices on the market. Then a more significant decline may begin around the 2030s. Nuclear energy will make a significant contribution to the world's electricity production by then, but it takes 15 years to build and commission new nuclear plants, so the window of opportunity is already tight. This assumes that no further disasters have occurred to make the world renounce nuclear energy altogether.

The move towards renewable sources of energy is well under way and will gather pace. Sun, wind and tides will be harnessed. It seems unlikely that politicians will give a lead in this. Their time horizon normally reaches only to the date of the next election. The move towards 'greenness' came from environmentalist pressure groups, not politicians. The latter became green when they realised that there were votes in being seen to be green.

34 USING THE THEORY AT WORK

So far this book has been about how the theory of time and energy explains the actions of individuals and nations past, present and future. Can the theory be used in the everyday environment of work?

For years manufacturers and distributors have sought to reduce the amount of time required to achieve a given measure of output. The energy required, whether human or non-human, was always taken into account. Factories replaced cottage industries and agricultural machinery replaced labourers.

The substitution of manual effort by machinery will continue in any economic system until the cost of the machinery, both its capitalised energy cost and its current energy consumption becomes greater than the cost of human energy.

The importance of the relationship between time and energy needs to be clearly understood in service industries, whether they are for profit of not. The amount of time that any person in an organisation spends on a task must be measured against the output he produces. A simple example illustrates this.

In days of typewriters, if a manager asked a secretary to retype a letter containing mistakes, the task was doubled. The value of the finished product might have been aesthetically more pleasing but its value as a means of communication had not been improved compared with manual corrections. The secretary commonly would not retype the letter but would make the corrections using Tipp-Ex. If today the same corrections are done by word-processor, the additional time required by the typist may be a small percentage of the time taken to type the original document, so doing the corrections and reprinting the letter are justified.

The amount of personal energy that office workers use today is negligible so every decision in an office can be guided by the following criteria:

a)   how much additional *time* will be spent/saved by any change in what I propose to do?

b)   what is the value of that time measured in wages and other employment costs?

c)   what will be the tangible (preferably measurable) benefits or disbenefits that will accrue to the organisation from the change?

d)   do the people affected by the change have an incentive in relation to their personal time and energy to accept the change?

Again, the example of the typist, the typewriter and the word-processor can be used. A typist who perceives that a word-processor will save 95% of the time in correcting a letter will welcome a word-processor even though learning to use it will entail an investment of time. The organisation benefits through obtaining more letters of high quality from the typist in a given amount of time. The increased output must exceed the cost of the word-processor to justify buying it.

Decisions about performance

Every person at work, at all times and relating to every action, should ask himself the question: how much time will this activity take and is that amount of time justified? In many cases we do not ask ourselves this question. "I have always done it this way...It is part of my job specification...If I don't do it, I shall be criticised". All these are standard responses that allow us to avoid the key question.

People who are self-employed have no such problem. Their time is their own. If they decide to do any activity, it is because they wish to use or to save their time in that way. An employed person's attitude depends on the value that he places on his personal time. If he can achieve a given output, say 20 sales visits per week which is his sales quota, he may prefer to go home early rather than increase his output. For this reason, sales people usually have commission as part of their earnings package.

Every individual must decide how he prefers to allocate his time between work and leisure. For most people, a working week entails at least 40 or more hours away from the home. 35 - 40 hours are spent doing the job, and the balance consists of meal breaks and commuting.

At two extremes, economic man can be classified as either *workaholic* or *work-abstainer*. A workaholic is not necessarily virtuous, greedy for money or ambitious. Many a workaholic does extra hours without being paid for them. He may do them because he is committed to the organisation or to his vocation. Equally he may do so because he is inefficient and spends too much time on trivial tasks. He may even do them because he has little social life, so his work takes the place of leisure.

A work-abstainer is not necessarily lazy or unmotivated. He may place a higher value than others on time with his family, playing golf or on other leisure activities.

Both the workaholic and the work-abstainer make judgements about how much time they wish to give to their employer or, if self-employed, to their business. Giving more time may mean earning more money, but not always. Giving less time may mean earning less money, but not always. Many manual workers are paid directly in accordance with the number of hours they work with overtime paid at a higher hourly rate. For them, the overtime hours are usually allocated by their managers rather than chosen, so a manual worker who does long hours is not necessarily a workaholic.

Self-employed people are self-motivated. Employed people have to be motivated in different ways. The key to managing people is first to see where they lie on the scale between being workaholics and work-abstainers. They can then be motivated to produce their best output for the institution in different ways. A workaholic can be motivated by promotion prospects or bonuses; a work-abstainer by the offer of additional days holiday.

For sales people, the results are generally easy to measure. For many other office workers and service providers, it less easy but still possible to define measures of output. In general, for every employee there should be goals defined in terms of quantity and quality of results achieved. An accounts clerk might be expected to process, say, 100 invoices a day (quantity) and to ensure that all were completed within five working days of receipt (quality). Once the goals have been set, the amount of time taken by the employee is of much less relevance than the achievement of the goals. The concept of flexible working hours should be considered when the output goals have been set and should entail a minimum and a maximum number to be worked rather than just the choice of when they are worked. A manager should be as critical of a person who works too many hours as of one who works too few.

Amount of time taken to make decisions
Doing things takes time. So does making decisions about what needs to be done. Decision making sometimes falls to a single person. Commonly, the more important the decision, the more people need to be involved in making it. This is recognised in most organisations and they set financial limits to the decisions that may be made by individual employees at different levels.

Every employee has an hourly cost rate to the institution and all should be aware of their own cost rate and roughly that of their colleagues. This need not mean that they know their colleagues' individual earnings, but they should know the average hourly cost for the grade. Armed with this knowledge, a person can make better decisions about the allocation of his time. "I cost the company £30 per hour, which includes all the overheads. I have just taken half an hour to compose a report. Did report justify it? Would a telephone call taking five minutes have achieved the same result?"

This approach is valuable at meetings. A thoughtful chairman might begin the meeting by saying: "there are five of us here. Our average individual hourly cost is £30 and I have scheduled two hours for this meeting. The overt cost of the meeting is therefore £300. That figure should be doubled to allow for the hidden costs of the meeting, namely the preparation of the papers, writing minutes and travel to the meeting, so the real cost is £600. Any decisions made at this meeting must justify that amount of time spent on them."

Meetings should be about conveying information and making decisions. The value of both is generally difficult to quantify in money terms. However, certain gains or losses will result from the decisions made. The appointments of staff, the purchase of equipment, or a decision to move premises all have major financial repercussions whereas an activity report providing background only may have little.

At meetings consisting of the provision of information and of making decisions, a variant of the 80/20 rule should be applied: 80 per cent of the time available should be applied to decisions; 20 per cent of the time should be used for discussion and information that do not lead to a decision at the meeting itself.

Responsibility for the performance of others
Every organisation is hierarchical in some degree. In most the rank of each person is known and the lines of responsibility are clear. In the army, a captain is always junior to a major who is junior to a colonel, and so on. Most people, though not all, seek promotion up the hierarchy. The overt rewards are more status and more money. Less obvious is the fact that promotion entails more control over time and energy, both human and physical. Discretionary spending power increases with seniority. The power to give instructions to subordinates is the power to control the way in which they apply their

time and energy.

Promotion or other forms of reward should never be made on the basis of whether a person is a workaholic or a work-abstainer but rather on the output achieved in relation to the job's goals. Other factors also must be taken into consideration, notably how well the person fits into the team. A good manager gets most from his staff by encouraging them to work the agreed hours fully and efficiently and then by measuring and comparing the output of each.

Any group of people working together has a common goal. That goal varies widely according to the reason that they are in the group. A company exists to make profits because without profits it ceases to trade. A non-profit organisation exists in order to achieve defined goals, for example the raising of a certain sum for charity. However, even within the non-profit organisation it is necessary to balance the financial books otherwise jobs are lost. It is as painful to be made redundant from a non-profit organisation as from a company, so holding to one's job and justifying the salary is a primary aim of economic man whatever the organisation within which he works.

Whatever the mission of the organisation, the essential way to ensure its highest level of effectiveness is by minimising the time spent by each member on achieving a defined goal. This is easier said than done but it is the obverse of Parkinson's famous law that says that any given task is expanded to fill the time available.

35   USING THE THEORY IN PRIVATE LIFE

Individuals' perceptions of the value of their time and energy vary. Among readers of this book there may be some who feel that they have all the time they need to achieve what they want to give to life or to take from it. They are lucky. Others find that there are many things that do not get done for lack of time and energy.   The remainder of this chapter is addressed to them.

Three keys to using time and energy effectively are
-       setting priorities;
-       doing tasks methodically; and
-       when possible, completing one activity before beginning the next.

Many books have been written on time management.   These primarily concern time at work and are intended to help people achieve more in a given amount of time and to do so while avoiding strain. Less has been written about planning leisure time and even less about planning the remainder of a lifetime. What follows is a simple way of enabling you to assess your fundamental priorities and better plan the use of your time and energy.

The permanent invalid test
The concept of this test is to help you get your priorities in life into perspective. Imagine the following circumstances.

You have had a short illness from which you now have recovered. However, the doctor says you are in a period of remission after which you will rapidly deteriorate and be permanently bed ridden. You will be in full possession of your mind, memories and emotions. He regrets that he cannot say how long your present remission will last, but typically it may be

1)   one month
2)   one year or
3)   five years at the most.

One important constraint is added to the test. The doctor tells you that you will need full time care as soon as remission is over. The cost of full time care will be £500 per week until you die.

The test is to ask yourself carefully not just once, but on a regular basis, what you will you do now in the light of this news?

A question may help you to gain clarity:

-      now that you know your active life is to be drastically shortened, what have been your most joyful memories and most profound regrets?

In the test the duration of normal life available to you is limited by the three possible horizons. Your energy, both personal and stored in the form of money and other assets, remains as now. The three questions make you differentiate between your short term, medium and longer term goals. Let us consider them in turn.

Case 1 – invalidity starts in a month

In this case the value of time becomes dramatically enhanced. Most people would stop work in order to be able to spend time with their nearest and dearest mingled with doing the things they like most.

Stopping work will not necessarily be a reflection of the nature of the job but rather the recognition that nothing is of the higher importance than human relationships. Those who would stop work simply to play golf or garden for the last month without any need for special time with other people must realise that they have failed in their human relationships and may be little missed whenever and however they go. Scrooge was able to change his attitude to human relationships within the space of a night. For most people doing so requires much more than one month.

Case 2 - invalidity in a year
With just one year before you the value of time becomes greatly enhanced though less so than in case 1. The most important decision is likely to be: do I stop work? If you continue to work for the final year, it shows that your job is of more importance to you than just earning money and this is a healthy sign. If, conversely under case 2, you would stop your job at once this suggests that you may need to rebalance your life to take account of personal relationships and putting your life in order for when you will be invalided.

Case 3 - invalidity in five years
For many, five years of remission might seem to be a reasonable period in which we would be unlikely to alter our way of life dramatically. There will still be the mortgage and the other household bills to pay. Also, our savings will become important to pay for our future care, so these may need to be built up or at least not depleted. However, many individual goals can realistically be achieved in five years and if we have only five years rather than our normal life-span, we are more likely to pursue these goals with energy, whether they be economic, spiritual or sexual.

Taken together, the *invalidity test* may give you clarity on how to lead your life even though the length of your life remains unknown. The test makes you take stock of your goals and your achievements, past and present. Most importantly they make you focus on your personal relationships and your goals using your available time and energy in achieving them.

The invalidity test makes you assess your priorities as an integrated economic, spiritual and sexual person. The test makes you aware of the finite nature of personal time and energy which we continually overlook in the hustle and bustle of coping with each day as it comes. The invalidity test is helpful in showing you where you currently are on the three dimensions: economic, spiritual and sexual.

If, in setting your priorities under any of the three cases, you decide you have to improve your relationships with family, colleagues at work or friends, this represents your spiritual dimension. If you decide that your priority is to buy the car of your dreams, this represents your economic dimension. If you decide that you will have a fling with some beguiling man or woman, this of course represents your sexual dimension. The invalidity test shows you which of your three dimensions is currently least well satisfied. Satisfying it should improve your pleasure in living whether you in fact are killed in a car-crash next week or die peacefully in your sleep aged 90.

The thought of permanent invalidity is so disturbing that some readers may disregard the test entirely, pointing out that the number of people who are paralysed in this way is very few. On the other hand, we all know people who have been in a car crash or have died early with motor neuron disease.

Death does not mean oblivion. There is much evidence, discussed in chapter 2, of life after death and of awareness at the time of death of the past. We have some control of the time allotted to us. For example, smoking and obesity are known to shorten life. We have some control of the personal energy allotted to us. Being healthy and of the right weight enable us to increase our personal energy. And we have significant control over how we allocate our time and personal energy until we become invalids or die.

When we come to the point in our lives at which little time and energy remain, it is certain that we shall feel happier and more accepting if we know that our true priorities have determined what we have thought, said and done in the past. Then, in the words of Edith Piaf's song, *je ne regrette rien, rien de rien.*

36 SPIRITUAL MAN TO THE RESCUE?

In the first part of this book I defined man using three dimensions: economic, spiritual and sexual. Most of this book has concerned economic man. The last years of the 20th century were momentous and reflected the triumph of economic man over dogma. The collapse of socialism in eastern Europe occurred with miraculously little blood-shed. The numbers who died in each of the revolutions in East Germany, Poland, Hungary, Czechoslovakia, Romania and other former communist states could be counted in hundreds, not thousands.

The death toll in the Arab spring initially was also quite low until the civil war to overthrow Colonel Gaddafi which was more protracted and violent. The unfinished civil war in Syria continues to inflict mounting suffering and casualties, both military and civilian, and has displaced a million or more Syrians who have fled across the border to Jordan. On August 21, 2013 gas was used by government forces with huge casualties among civilians in a suburb of Damascus held by the rebels.

In the cities of the western world civil peace is fragile. Outbreaks of disorder take ethnic lines. Minorities, usually black or south Asian, express anger at what they feel to be discrimination. Indigenous citizens feel threatened and form anti-migrant groups. Immigration that consists of too many people too soon provides the underlying cause for simmering anger and mistrust among those who are hostile to immigrants. They resent what they see as their failure to conform to the standards of the society where they come to live. They perceive immigrants as taking social housing, jobs, free health treatment and state benefits.

The conviction of Asian paedophile gangs in the UK and the murder of Drummer Rigby have heightened tensions. Some native Britons see the wearing of the burka by Muslim women as divisive and threatening. The rise of jihadism coupled with bomb plots is feared and with justification. The creation of Sharia courts within Muslim communities threatens the long established British judicial system. Within the indigenous majority economic man feels threatened and reacts primitively.

To set against the sporadic violence in west European countries and the continuing ferment in the Arab world there is a resurgence of activity by spiritual man. Charitable agencies proliferate doing good works at home and abroad. Floods in Bangladesh, famine in Africa, earthquakes in South America and refugees in Syria elicit massive humanitarian response in which spiritual man is the driving force.

It would be easy but wrong to equate spiritual man with good and economic man with evil. It is the drive of economic man, selfish though it may be, that discovered how to harness the planet's massive resources of energy and other assets to the benefit of us all. Without the persistence of economic man the world in its entirety would still be in the stone age. The mistake the world is making is to rely on economic man to resolve all problems as though they were economic problems only.

Can spiritual man come to the world's aid in time? First, we must rule out the possibility of goodness being imposed upon mankind, for example by the second coming of Jesus Christ. To assume an imminent second coming is to remove from mankind the need to work towards our own salvation. The first step must be towards promoting genuine democracy through voting at every level, from local and national government, through international agencies and up to the United Nations.

It is evident from the history of the past 100 years that wars are more easily begun by dictatorships. Dictatorship is impossible in a true democracy because politicians can be removed by the ballot instead of the bullet. Democracy does not ensure the resurgence of spiritual man but is it the best defence against excessive inequalities and poverty that economic man may advocate or condone. Democracy must be made to thrive. In every organisation of whatever size and paid for from public funds, there must be the power to elect and remove those in authority by means of voting. The voting system itself must be one which guarantees the proportional power of minorities.

How can we give spiritual man more say in the running of society? The home and education must be the answer. I do not believe that all babies are born with original sin. However, they may inherit a predisposition either to sin or to goodness just as they may inherit their parents' physical appearance and other characteristics. Home and schools must become imbued with the values of spiritual man. Schools must be seen as teaching the values of spiritual man, specifically tolerance and peace, as well as the knowledge and skills needed by economic man.

Implanting the values and attitudes of spiritual man into the home and educational systems will take generations. Time is not on our side. The first essential must be the creation of a non-violent society. By law, no-one should be permitted to strike another person. Parents should not be allowed to strike their children. Sports entailing the intentional infliction of pain on man or beast should be banned: boxing, hunting and bull-fighting have no place in a civilised society. Films and images depicting violence should be self-censored willingly by the media. The possession of weapons of violence, guns and knives, should be punishable severely.

Culprits must be made to pay compensation to victims and to society. Community service is the right way of doing so. Prison should be used only for violent criminals to protect the public.

Non-violence is not the same thing as love of mankind and the environment, but it creates the possibility of a society and a world without violence and fear. Without fear, weapons of destruction, whether bombs, firearms or knives, become unnecessary for attack or defence.

In this book, I have shown how economic man dominates the world we live in and has largely subordinated spiritual and sexual man in matters that concern our daily lives. The planet's past and present reflect that domination. Its future depends on establishing the authority of spiritual man.

Lightning Source UK Ltd.
Milton Keynes UK
UKOW06f1528100516

273956UK00001B/27/P